Dance of Heavenly Bliss

Divine Inspiration for Humanity

by

Garnet Schulhauser

For permission, serialization, condensation, adaptions, or for our catalog of other publications, write to Ozark Mountain Publishing, Inc., P.O. box 754, Huntsville, AR 72740, ATTN: Permissions Department.

Library of Congress Cataloging-in-Publication Data

Schulhauser, Garnet, 1951 -

Dance of Heavenly Bliss by Garnet Schulhauser

This is the third book and it continues the saga of the author's spiritual awakening that began when he was confronted on the street by a homeless man named Albert who turned out to be a wise spirit in disguise--an emissary from the spirit world. The author recounts more astral adventures with Albert who took him to meet several distinguished souls on the Spirit Side, including Moses, Jesus and his mother Mary, Lucifer, and the goddess Athena. In the Akashic Records, he got to view an ancient human civilization that lived among the dinosaurs, the building of Stonehenge with the help of visitors from the stars, and the crash of the alien spacecraft in Roswell in 1947.

1. Spirit Guides 2. Reincarnation 3. Life After Death 4. Metaphysics

I. Schulhauser, Garnet, 1951 – II. Reincarnation III. Metaphysics IV. Title

Library of Congress Catalog Card Number: 2015957999

ISBN: 9781940265322

Cover Design: noir33.com
Book set in: Californian FB and Attend
Book Design: Tab Pillar
Published by:

PO Box 754
Huntsville, AR 72740
800-935-0045 or 479-738-2348 fax: 479-738-2448
WWW.OZARKMT.COM

Printed in the United States of America

To Rudy, Rita, Lloyd, and Margaret

Endorsements

After reading Garnet Schulhauser's book *Dance of Heavenly Bliss*, and I am struck by his desire to improve humanity and his contact with Spirit, something that is obviously important to him. In many ways, with Albert as his guide, he has expressed his love for creatures on our planet, for humanity, and for the universe. Anybody who wishes to have a good read and an interesting journey in spirit should take this book and spend time to peruse the expressions given about the spirit world in order to make up their own minds on many questions that they have asked about the Other Side.

Well done, Garnet, for taking the time to provide humanity with alternative thoughts. Not everybody has the bravery that is required to express the differing opinions on the spirit world to the masses.

—**Katherine Bright ND,** host of **News for the Soul Radio** (www.katherinebrightaustralia.com)

In *Dance of Heavenly Bliss*, Albert's newest revelations are infused with an added sense of urgency. Garnet Schulhauser's Spirit Guide Albert showcases a sobering outlay of worldly events/higher consciousness prompts, suggesting our lifestyle and sustainability are at odds. It becomes all too clear that Mama Earth and our planetary cohabitants are in desperate need for humans to exit our adolescent phase ... and soon.

—**Wendy Garrett,** host of **Conscious Living Radio** (http://bit.ly/1CO3Go7)

With gentle humor and firm guidance from his spirit companion, Albert, Garnet Schulhauser's new book takes an unflinching look at the ways in which we live out of alignment with our planet and our soul path. Offering a wake-up call of hope and inspiration, *Dance of Heavenly Bliss* is an inspiring read for those who seek a deeper connection with Spirit and who want to be part of a positive energetic shift that could transform life as we know it.

—**Karen Hager,** intuitive guide & host of **Out of the Fog Radio** (http://www.karenhager.com)

Garnet's new book, *Dance of Heavenly Bliss*, is one of the most profound and thought-provoking books I have ever read! The book contains information that is nothing less than a gift to humanity on why we are here, and what is the purpose of life. With channeled messages from his spirit guide (Albert), the book provides an extremely unique and valuable insight into reincarnation, the purpose of life, the life plan, the life review, and provides, (according to Albert), "... inspiration and comfort to humans searching for meaning in their lives..."

Garnet was guided to write this wonderful book by his spirit guide, Albert, who took him on a series of out-of-body trips to meet several distinguished souls on the Spirit Side, including Moses, Jesus and his mother Mary, Lucifer, and the goddess Athena. In the Akashic Records, he got to view an ancient human civilization that lived among the dinosaurs, the building of Stonehenge with the help of visitors from the stars, and the crash of the alien spacecraft in Roswell in 1947. These astral trips included visits to other planets with human civilizations that are much different from our own, including one with a matriarchal society ruled by women, as well as a frightening encounter with a Black Hole in the center of our galaxy.

I urge everyone to read this book because of its important messages, which could help transform this planet into a beautiful world that is based on love, harmony, and peace – rather than hate, anger, and war... The white light is always much stronger than the dark. And I know the forces of light will win out against the forces of darkness, and I believe that there is a very bright and wonderful future for all of us!

—**Ted Mahr**, psychic and host of **Out of this World Radio** (www.outofthisworld1150.com) and host of the **Galactic Wisdom Conference**, bringing the best UFO, psychic, and spiritual healers to the Seattle, USA area annually every spring (www.galacticwisdomconference.com)

In his third book, *Dance of Heavenly Bliss*, Garnet Schulhauser continues the saga of his spiritual enlightenment with his spirit guide, Albert. During his astral excursions with his guide, the author conversed with Gaia (Mother Earth) and travelled to other planets with human civilizations, including an advanced matriarchal world ruled by women. And on his frequent visits to the Spirit Side, Garnet interviewed many famous and infamous souls, like Moses and Jesus—who regaled him with tales of their lives on Earth. This book is a riveting spiritual exposé designed to encourage humans to embrace love for one another and for Mother Earth and all of her creatures. It is uplifting and a joy to read, and highly recommended for anyone who yearns for more love and peace on our beautiful planet!

–**Karen Noé**, host of **Angel Quest Radio** and Hay House author of **Your Life After Their Death: A Medium's Guide to Healing After a Loss** (http://www.karennoe.com/)

Dance of Heavenly Bliss is yet another outstanding offering by author, Garnet Schulhauser. Inspiring and riveting, Garnet, via his spirit guide Albert, allows each of us to vicariously participate on his many excursions that serve to expand our conscious awareness. No stone is left unturned as he offers fresh perspective on age-old mysteries that currently persist in our time both on and off our magnificent earth. If one is seeking spiritual expansion; if one is looking for new perspectives on ancient concepts, then this book is definitely a must-read.

—**Ara Parisien**, International Psychic Medium, Spiritual Teacher, and host
of **Virtual Vision FM**
(http://virtualvisionfm.com/)

Balance in all things. This new book from Garnet Schulhauser, *Dance of Heavenly Bliss*, focuses us to a wakeup call of huge proportions. As we travel with Garnet and Albert we begin to see where we have gone off course as a species and how this has adversely affected the place we call home, Gaia, Earth, Our Mother. The story line may not sooth the reader but I do not think it is supposed to. This book is a pointed notification to humanity, a call to action to stop just wringing our hands over the plight of the planet we live on and to do something to help it revert to the sustaining life force that it was originally intended to be.

As you continue to travel with Albert and Garnet, you will meet souls that you would like to talk to and get to eavesdrop on their conversations about why they did some of the things they did and what happened to them because and in spite of those actions. Garnet asks the tough, perplexing questions and some of the answers he gets may surprise you, BUT I guarantee you will also be enlightened. By reliving the experiences of the lives of these souls, the famous, infamous and nondescript, you will be given a new appreciation and tolerant understanding of just what it truly means to be a soul living a human experience both for others and yourself.

—**Chessie Roberts**, host of **Get on the Grid Radio** and author of **Evolving into Self, From the Puppet to the Master: My Evolution from the Cradle to the Grid**
(www.ChessieRoberts.com)

Acknowledgments

There are many people I would like to acknowledge for their encouragement, inspiration, and support in connection with the writing and publishing of *Dance of Heavenly Bliss.*

First, a well-deserved thank you to Julia, Nancy, and Shonda, and all the staff at Ozark Mountain Publishing, for their assistance throughout the process.

I am grateful for all the messages I received from friends, family, and fans of *Dancing on a Stamp* and *Dancing Forever with Spirit* who encouraged me to write this sequel so they could read about my new astral adventures with Albert. I truly appreciate all the positive feedback I have been receiving.

And many thanks for the support I received from all the spiritually enlightened people I met along the way: my fellow authors at Ozark Mountain Publishing and all the gracious and charming radio-show hosts who interviewed me on their shows. It has been comforting for me to enjoy the company of so many like-minded people.

Contents

Chapter One
Albert Returns

Monday morning reared its ugly head once again. My eyes blinked open to see the sunlight streaming through my bedroom window. The red LED numerals on the bedside clock displayed 5:30, so I closed my eyes, hoping to catch a few more minutes of sleep. I could hear the juncos singing outside of the open window, and I wondered how these little creatures could be so happy at this time of the morning.

When sleep did not return I slid out of bed and made my way to the bathroom, where I stared at my mug in the mirror as I rubbed the electric shaver over my stubbly beard. *Why did God invent Mondays?* I wondered. *Why couldn't every day be a Friday?*

I knew the days of the week did not exist on the Spirit Side—a wonderful thought indeed. Someday I would return to the Spirit Side to enjoy the timeless bliss in our Home beyond the veil. But I had to finish my journey on Earth before I could return.

My mission today was to begin writing my third book, and I hoped Albert would show up to provide me with some much-needed inspiration. I dearly missed the wit and wisdom of Albert, who had disappeared several months ago—leaving a huge gap in my life.

Albert is one of my spirit guides and the star of my first two books, *Dancing on a Stamp* and *Dancing Forever with Spirit*. He is a wise old soul—an emissary from the spirit world—who appeared before me one day to answer all the "big questions" in life I had been pondering for many years.

As I described in *Dancing on a Stamp*, I first met Albert in 2007 when I was still practicing law. I was strolling down the street on a sunny day in May when a homeless man jumped out of the shadows to stop me in my tracks. This street person, who was Albert in disguise, looked like a typical homeless man, with long greasy hair, scraggly beard, and dirty clothes. My usual response to such encounters was to make a quick sidestep to go around, but this time I stood there like a deer caught in the headlights—transfixed by his radiant blue eyes that shone like two little blue stars.

His gaze penetrated deeply into my very being, right down to the depths of my soul, and I sensed he knew all the intimate details of my life: my hopes and aspirations, my fears and anxieties, and my deepest and darkest secrets. Despite feeling somewhat naked and exposed, I did not feel violated because at the same time his sparkling eyes sent a wave of pure unconditional love that infused my whole body with an unforgettable sense of peace and security. I could have stood there forever basking in this gush of love, but he broke the spell when he said, "Why are you here?" before promptly disappearing into a nearby store.

When I found Albert on the same street the next day, he told me he was a soul, just like me, who had come to answer my questions and help me on my journey. Initially I was skeptical, as he looked like he had been sleeping on the street for weeks, and he smelled like a dead fish. Fortunately my intuition prompted me to take a chance with this man—to see if he could really answer all the eternal questions I had been asking myself for years: *Who am I? Why am I here? What is the purpose of my life? What will happen to me after I die?*

So I sat down on the bench that day with this homeless man and our conversation began. I soon learned Albert was one of my spirit guides in disguise, and I was the only one who could see him as the homeless man. After our third meeting Albert no longer appeared in the flesh, and he spoke to me telepathically as a voice in my head.

Albert answered all my questions with wisdom and humor, and our conversations were lighthearted, like two friends chatting over a beer. His responses felt right and rang true in my heart, so I knew what he told me was the "real" truth.

I was surprised when he asked me to write a book about our conversations so all humans would have access to his revelations. At first I was reluctant to take on this task, because I had never before written a book. I soon learned, however, it was futile to argue with Spirit, so I wrote *Dancing on a Stamp* with helpful guidance from Albert.

Albert's revelations were often startling but always illuminating. Most of his truths flew in the face of almost everything Christian holy men had been preaching for centuries and contradicted many of the beliefs I had been taught as a child, growing up in a very religious Roman Catholic family. It soon became clear to me, however, that his truths made much more sense than the dogmas of the Catholic Church.

2

Albert revealed that we are all eternal souls who will live forever. Our natural home is the Spirit Side, a wonderful place filled with peace and joy, and we will return there after our physical bodies die. We were created by the Source (known to some as the Creator or God) as an individual aspect of the Source, and we are intimately connected to each other and to everything else in the universe. We are beings of energy that spun out from the Source like sparks of light from the central sun.

We incarnated as humans by our own choice—no one made us come to this planet. We came to Earth, which exists on a plane of dense matter, to learn and experience things that do not exist on the Spirit Side so we can grow and evolve as souls. Before we began our human incarnations we each prepared a Life Plan that set out the significant details and events of our proposed lives, including our names and places of birth, and the identities of our parents, siblings, spouses, children, and friends. We designed our Life Plans with a view to experiencing the events and learning the lessons needed to advance our evolution. But our Life Plans (the details of which we are not allowed to remember while on Earth) do not dictate everything that happens to us because we have free will to act and make decisions during our time on this planet.

Contrary to what most organized religions preach, the Source does not control the events in our lives, and it does not make rules for us to follow. Nothing we do is right or wrong in an absolute sense, and we cannot offend or disappoint the Source, which wants to experience the universe it created in all of its facets through our many different incarnations.

It follows that the Source will not judge or punish us for anything we did during our human incarnations. All souls return to the Spirit Side after their physical bodies die regardless of what they did on Earth, which means murderers and terrorists return to the Spirit Side just like all the good people. And we can incarnate on Earth over and over until we are satisfied we have evolved to the extent necessary to graduate from this school.

Albert described our true home, the Spirit Side, as a wonderful place permeated with unconditional love and free from pain, suffering, and all negative emotions. It is like the heaven described by many religions—a blissful place with many interesting challenges in the joyful pursuit of wisdom. Souls returning to the Spirit Side can choose to remain there indefinitely, return to Earth for another incarnation, or incarnate into one of the countless other life forms in the universe. Our souls are on a never-ending trek of exploration and evolution, a delightful voyage with no finish line.

Overall I found Albert's revelations to be comforting and inspiring, and I was honored he had asked me to recount them in *Dancing on a Stamp*. But my job as Albert's messenger was not over when I finished my first book, because he told me I had to write at least three more books. I groaned a little when he outlined his plans for me, although I knew resistance was futile. Even though I relished the prospect of renewed contact with Albert, the thought of writing more books was somewhat daunting. In the end I resigned myself to the task of writing my second book, as I waited patiently for Albert to provide me with more revelations from beyond the veil.

Dancing Forever with Spirit continued my saga with Albert, when he appeared in my bedroom one night as an ethereal spirit to escort me on a series of astral adventures to teach me more about our universe and the cycle of life on Earth. Albert believed a picture was worth a thousand words, and to that end he took me on a series of astral tours so I could describe in vivid detail his new revelations for the people on Earth. We explored a dazzling white city on the Spirit Side, other planets in the galaxy with intriguing life forms, and some of the far-flung regions of our planet that suffer from human abuse.

These fascinating out-of-body excursions included a visit to a water planet where the resident cetaceans implored humans to stop the carnage of their cousins on Earth, a rendezvous with a benevolent race of extraterrestrial beings who have been observing Earth for eons, and a trip to another dimension to observe the idyllic world of humans who have made the shift to the New Earth. With guidance from Albert, I gained access to the Akashic Records (which contain the history of every life in the universe) to view some gripping episodes from several of my previous lives that were often tragic but always enthralling, and to sneak a glimpse into the secret life of Jesus.

Albert taught me how to become better at hearing the subtle messages from my spirit guides and the secret to finding my life purpose. And as a special treat, Albert took me to visit one of the focal points of the Source—a Central Sun where I was immersed in a pool of love that made me feel totally at one with the universe, the ultimate sense of unity.

These nightly escapades with Albert were designed to rouse humans from their callous stupor by displaying some of the inexcusable abuse humans inflict on Mother Earth, the other creatures on our planet, and on other humans, with the hope we will renounce the dark side of humanity in favor of spiritual enlightenment.

Albert cautioned we must be extra vigilant at this stage of human development lest we let our negative emotions run amok and destroy all life on our planet. Albert said we can avoid this catastrophe (with a little help from our extraterrestrial friends and the good spirits who watch over us) by a concerted effort on our part to discard our guilt and fear (and all the other negative emotions that plague humanity) and embrace love and compassion for everyone and everything around us. If we proceed down this path, we will raise our vibrations and expand our consciousness in order to transition to the New Earth, where we will enjoy life filled with love, peace, and harmony.

Dancing Forever with Spirit was a call to action for humanity—a plea from Spirit for humans to wake up and stop the abuse caused by their actions and neglect and focus their energy on helping everyone make the shift to a higher dimension. If we do not act quickly and with firm resolve we might self-destruct like some earlier civilizations on our planet.

I very much enjoyed my time with Albert while I was writing my first two books, and I yearned for his return so I could once again tap into his boundless wisdom. While I had resigned myself to follow Albert's wishes and write another book, I needed Albert to lead the way. *Surely he must know I need his input*, I thought wishfully.

Albert was always full of surprises. He had first introduced himself to me as a flesh-and-bones homeless man, but later he appeared in astral form to take me on some amazing out-of-body adventures. How he would make his next appearance in my life was still a mystery to me, although I was confident he would return when the time was right. So all I had to do was hurry up and wait!

Albert did not keep me waiting for very long. A few days later he appeared once again in my bedroom in the dead of night—a ghost-like figure standing at the foot of my bed. He looked the same as before— an ethereal spirit in his homeless-man attire, grinning like a Cheshire cat. Without a word, he beckoned me to follow him as I had done many times before. This time I remembered the drill, so I reached out to grasp his outstretched hand as my astral body slipped easily out of my sleeping corporeal frame. I turned around to see my earthly body still sound asleep in my bed beside my wife and little dog, but I was not concerned as I knew I would be back before dawn. I nodded to Albert and followed him up through the ceiling and into the night sky, where we paused high above our beautiful planet.

I could not keep my curiosity bottled up any longer, so I sprung my questions on Albert. "How are things, Albert? And where have you been for the past few months?"

"I am doing just fine. I have been working with a group of souls who are planning to incarnate as humans for the first time. My goal was to warn them about the idiosyncrasies of the human mind and its tendency to churn through thousands of thoughts every day. They found this difficult to accept until I showed them how to follow people on Twitter. Then they could see for themselves how the human mind was capable of spewing forth so many random and meaningless thoughts in a very short period of time.

"Now that I have finished tutoring this group, I must continue with my mission to disseminate messages from Spirit, which is why I approached you again tonight. I want to show you a few things you can include in your third book."

"It is nice to see you again," I responded. "I am eager to learn more about the cycle of life on Earth and elsewhere in the universe, and I am sure you have many more eye-opening vistas to show me. I know you want me to see the things that will serve to deliver your message to humanity, but in the past I often found them to be shocking and distressful. When will you take me on a fun trip?"

"I suppose I could take you to *Disneyland*, although it wouldn't be much fun when you are in astral form—you would miss out on eating too many hot dogs and then puking all over your shoes. Or how about Las Vegas? Except you wouldn't be able to play the slot machines because you can't take any money with you when traveling out of your body. So you see, astral traveling can be a real bummer at times."

"Especially with you as the tour guide, Albert. You told me before humor is alive and well on the Spirit Side, but I fear you must have been snoozing when the Source was doling out the wit."

"Touché," Albert responded with a mischievous grin. "I promise you will get to choose the destinations at some point in the future, but for now I must ask you to follow my itinerary. Spirit has an agenda for you and your fellow humans, and it is important you work with us for the betterment of your civilization. You must be patient and eventually your mission will be over, and then you will be able to enjoy the rest of your journey on Earth."

"I thought you were going to say that, Albert, but it was worth a try. Where would you like to take me this time?"

"To begin," Albert continued, "we need to meet once again with the Council of Wise Ones. They have something important to tell you."

We floated through the shimmering doorway to the Spirit Side, and we strolled through the lush green meadow I remembered from previous trips. Once again I could enjoy the fragrant scents wafting up from the flowers bordering the path, resplendent with a profusion of iridescent hues that were indescribably beautiful. The songbirds perched on the cherry trees filled the glen with their joyful rhapsody. The majestic oak trees at the far edge of the meadow stood at attention, their leaves fluttering in the gentle breeze. The scene was exquisite beyond words, and I felt a lump in my throat as I surveyed the sublime tableau spread out before us.

I followed Albert to the top of a gentle slope where I could see in the distance the towers and spires of the white city known as Aglaia. I had been here before with Albert, although I still marveled at its opulence, with its palatial structures glimmering in the soft light that seemed to emanate from everywhere. We entered the city through its large stately portal and strolled down the wide boulevard.

The streets were full of people gathered in small groups and engaged in animated conversation, while others sauntered casually with the carefree confidence that sprang from a life of peace and security. As before, I was captivated by the display of diverse and vibrant attire worn by the denizens of this magnificent city.

Albert had explained on my first visit to Aglaia that souls on the Spirit Side could choose to appear in any form they pleased, and they would often assume the appearance of someone from one of their previous incarnations on Earth. This explained the diversity of the apparel proudly worn by these beautiful souls: tuxedos from the Gatsby era, long silk evening gowns from seventeenth-century France, miniskirts from the sixties, kangas from Africa, gauchos from Argentina, fustanellas from the Balkans, and chimas from Korea, just to mention a few.

Eventually we arrived at the majestic Hall of Wisdom, with magnificent white Grecian pillars lining the front. We entered through the arched doorway and made our way down the broad corridor until we reached an elegant burnished brass door. I remembered from a previous trip with Albert that the Hall of Wisdom was the home of the Council of Wise Ones, which was a committee of very wise old souls whose primary function was to oversee all the incarnations on Earth.

Albert tapped gently with the round doorknocker before we entered the Council chamber on the other side. It looked the same as my first visit with the Council of Wise Ones (described in *Dancing Forever with Spirit*): a circular room with a high domed ceiling and a large table in the center in the shape of a semicircle. Seated around the table were the eleven members of the Council wearing long gold robes tied at the waist with white sashes, looking even more regal than before. The august lady seated at the center, who had introduced herself as Sophia, was once again the chair of the Council.

"Welcome back, Garnet," Sophia began in her soft and dignified manner. "We have been looking forward to this meeting as we have something important to tell you. Before we begin, please tell us how you are enjoying your adventures with Albert."

"Albert has been a great tour guide," I responded. "All of the vistas I saw with Albert were fascinating and thought provoking, although I was shocked and dismayed by some of the scenes of abuse I was allowed to witness. I understand these trips were carefully orchestrated for my benefit, so I could write about them in my book."

"Indeed, your astral adventures were designed to inspire your writing, and we thank you for describing them in your second book. We have more information to pass on to you today, and then Albert will take you on a few more excursions which we hope will serve as inspiration for your third book.

"We are unhappy with the progress humanity has been making on the road to spiritual enlightenment. Humans are still not able to control their negative emotions to the extent necessary to raise their vibratory rates and expand their consciousness, so they can make the shift to a higher dimension. Too many humans are ruled by fear rather than love, which fosters anger, hate, greed, and jealousy. This often results in violence and abuse toward other humans, other creatures on Earth, and Mother Earth herself.

"There have been previous human civilizations on Earth that had learned to reject fear and embrace love, and there are now civilizations on other planets and dimensions that have learned to live in peace and harmony with each other and the other creatures who share their world. If these enlightened societies have found a way to reject the dark side of humanity, your civilization should be able to do the same.

"Most humans on Earth are arrogant and self-centered, which is why so many people have little regard for your environment and the other creatures on your planet. The abuse humans dish out to animals is appalling, not to mention the manmade pollution that fouls your air, poisons your water, and desecrates your land. Mother Earth and her other creatures would be much better off if humans, in their present state, did not inhabit your planet.

"And the violence humans inflict on other humans of your planet is an absolute disgrace and not in keeping with what we would expect from a race of intelligent beings. Your civilization is a prime example of a race whose emotional intelligence has not kept up with its technological advances. And unless there is a drastic change in your thinking, your civilization could face a very tragic ending.

"But all is not lost because there are many humans who have seen the light and recognize the importance of living in harmony with Mother Earth and all of her inhabitants. The milk of human kindness flows freely in these people, and the love they radiate is a shining beacon for all to follow. The challenge for humanity is to increase this flow of love until it smothers all the darkness that pervades your planet.

"Your mission is to let Albert guide you on a journey of enlightenment to search for the truth about the cycle of life on your planet and elsewhere in your galaxy and to tap into the wisdom of some extraordinary souls who have riveting tales about life on Earth. Then you must reveal what you have learned for all to see."

"Farewell for now, Garnet. We will meet again soon. Enjoy your adventures with Albert."

We waved farewell to the Council and left the Hall of Wisdom, meandering through the throngs of people on the main boulevard. Before we reached the city exit, I stopped when I heard loud cheering and clapping coming from somewhere on my right. Albert could see I was curious about the applause, so he led me down one of the side streets in the direction of the clamor.

Soon we came upon a large open amphitheater nestled on the side of a hill. We were standing on the top level of the stadium looking down on the semicircle of seats, filled with thousands of spectators in colorful garb that stretched all the way down to the stage at the bottom. As we sat down on a nearby bench I noticed two individuals standing at the front of the stage, with an orchestra forming a semicircle behind them. Albert said the two performers were the souls who had last been on Earth as members of the Beatles, and the orchestra was composed of former members of the London Symphony Orchestra. I focused my gaze on the two men at the front, and my heart skipped a beat when I realized they did indeed look like John Lennon and George Harrison.

The orchestra soon launched into the soft strains of the next song, which I recognized immediately as one of the Beatles' number-one hits, "Norwegian Wood." When John and George chimed in with the vocals, the music was breathtaking—a magical tour de force that evoked many fond memories from my past. I stood there with a lump in my throat, totally captivated by their performance as they slid seamlessly from "Yesterday" to "Let It Be," followed by a stirring rendition of "Something." And when they closed the set with "Hey Jude," one of my all-time favorites, I could feel the shivers running down my spine as their adoring fans, who were all standing by now, belted out the chorus in a joyful salute to these talented musicians. It was mesmerizing, and I could have stayed there forever.

When the set was over Albert broke my reverie with a gentle nudge. Reluctantly, I followed him back to the main boulevard and out through the stately portal of the city.

"This was an amazing concert," I said. "Can we come back later to listen to the rest of it?"

"Concerts like this run on a continual basis on the Spirit Side, one of the pleasant aspects of living back at Home. We have a mission to fulfill, so the concerts will have to wait. Come with me, I want to show you something on your planet that will be appalling to most humans, but important for you to see firsthand."

I nodded my assent, knowing full well Albert would take me there even if I didn't want to go. *Let the adventure begin*, I thought as we floated down toward the beautiful blue planet we call Earth.

Chapter Two
A Whale's Tale

We floated down through the wispy cirrus clouds that drifted over large sections of North America, eventually touching down in a large aquarium in California. It was several hours before dawn, and the place was deserted except for a few security guards making their rounds.

Albert led me to the largest sea-water tank in the facility—the one that held the orcas (killer whales). At the edge of the pool I noticed a full-grown orca, its black-and-white markings gleaming in the bright moonlight. Albert waved and hailed the orca: "Greetings, Yolanda. As promised, I brought a human visitor in astral form to meet with you."

To my surprise, Yolanda responded telepathically: "Greetings to you, Albert, and to your human companion."

"I brought Garnet with me to hear your story, with the hope all humans will eventually understand the truth about captive whales."

"Let me start at the beginning," Yolanda continued. "I was born in the wild in the Pacific Northeast where I enjoyed the love and attention I got from my mother and the companionship of the other orcas in my pod. Life was good for my first three years, and I very much enjoyed frolicking in the clear blue waters of the Pacific. But then one day my life was turned upside down when I was captured by humans and wrenched from my family.

"I was taken to this aquarium and left alone in this tank. Although I was fed well and cared for by the attentive staff, I dearly missed my pod and the freedom of the open sea. Four years ago I gave birth to my first calf who was shipped off to another aquarium as soon as he was weaned from my milk. I will not ever see him again, and he will likely never feel the joy of freedom that I once had.

"The trainers here are kind to me, even if they insist on teaching me silly tricks to amuse the multitudes of people who visit the aquarium every year. They are smug with satisfaction when I master a new trick, without realizing I knew at the outset exactly what they wanted me to do. I pretend to learn slowly so they will think I am smart, but not as smart as they are.

"I have tried in vain to communicate telepathically with these humans, but to no avail. They have not yet learned to unleash the power of their minds to allow for this discourse, which is unfortunate for all the creatures on this planet. If they could hear what I am telling you now, they would not keep us on display in this concrete prison.

"I remain in contact with the whales who freely roam the oceans, and I envy their existence. I am also aware of the harm and abuse humans have inflicted on my brethren in the past, which still continues today in several parts of the world. And it is not only whales, but dolphins, sharks, and many other species of sea life that are hunted and killed by your race every day, or who perish from entanglement with fishing lines and nets deployed by humans who seem to have little or no regard for the creatures of the sea.

"Humans seem to think the other creatures of this planet have no feelings or emotions, are not self-aware, and were put on this planet solely for the pleasure of humankind. They don't respect our intelligence because we have not developed any technology, as they seem to believe advanced technology is an essential part of superior intelligence. This couldn't be further from the truth, as you will come to understand on your trips with Albert.

"It is difficult for us to comprehend the unbridled arrogance of humans in their treatment of other creatures on Earth. While we acknowledge that some of your kind are empathetic to our plight and strive to stop the abuse, there are still far too many humans who don't know or don't care about our predicament. Why can't humans learn to live in harmony with Mother Earth and all of her creatures?

"I pray one day they will set me free to roam the ocean with my pod as I did years ago, but I am afraid I will die before this happens. I can only hope it will not be too late for my son and all the other creatures held in your watery prisons."

I could feel the strong emotions emanating from this magnificent creature, and tears welled up in my eyes as I listened to her tale of woe. If all other humans on this planet could hear this story, I know drastic changes would occur, and we would stop the abuse we inflict on the other creatures of our planet.

"Thank you, Yolanda, for baring your soul to me. I will do my best to propagate your message to my fellow humans. Hopefully this will lead to drastic changes in the way humans regard other animals on this planet."

My visit with Yolanda reminded me of my astral excursion to the planet Proteus (which I described *in Dancing Forever with Spirit*) where I met two of its resident creatures, a humpback whale and a dolphin, who implored me to help their cousins on Earth. Seeing and hearing Yolanda in this aquarium served to reinforce their plea for help and increased my resolve to do whatever I could to help them.

I bade farewell to Yolanda and followed Albert back to our rendezvous point high above Earth. I glanced anxiously at Albert, apprehensive about where he might take me next. I understood his agenda for me was intended to be informative, but some of his trips were emotionally draining. I could only wish Albert would let me return to that delightful concert beyond the veil.

But Albert had other plans for me. "I am taking you back down to your planet to show you a couple of scenes of abuse that may make you sick to your stomach. Are you ready?"

I nodded feebly, bracing myself for the worst.

Chapter Three

Appalling Abuse

With a grim face, Albert motioned for me to follow as he drifted down toward the East Coast of America where we landed in an urban park in the center of a busy metropolis. It was a sunny Saturday morning, and the park was filled with people sitting on benches or sprawled out on the lush green grass. Several groups of teenagers were playing catch with a Frisbee, while the younger children gamboled cheerfully on the playground equipment. There were mothers pushing their babies in strollers and seniors moving slowly with halting steps behind their walkers. And almost everyone was smiling as they soaked up the warm sunshine.

I trailed Albert to a pond near the north edge of the park. I noticed a young boy, maybe seven or eight, playing with his little dog—a cocker spaniel with a shiny jet-black coat. Albert said the boy's name was Riley and his beloved dog was Rascal. Riley's dad sat on a nearby bench, his attention focused on his smart phone.

Riley and Rascal were enjoying their favorite game, which called for Rascal to chase and fetch a tennis ball tossed by Riley with the aid of a ball thrower. They both took great delight in this game, and neither seemed to lose interest even after more than an hour of play. All was well until Riley threw the ball over the top of a hedge near the edge of the park. Rascal scampered after the ball and was forced to go around the hedge to find it. When Rascal did not return with the ball, Riley ran behind the hedge to find his pet, but Rascal was nowhere to be seen. After several minutes of frantic calling, Jimmy fetched his dad, and they both spent the next hour scouring the park and the nearby streets for their little dog. But Rascal had disappeared. Reluctantly, a sobbing Riley returned home with his dad, vowing to return the next day to continue the search.

From my vantage point I could see what had happened. The tennis ball had landed beside a young man, David, leaning up against his van. As Rascal screamed around the hedge in pursuit of the ball, David crouched down and picked it up. Then he waved the ball in his hand to get Rascal's attention before setting it down on the grass. Rascal approached tentatively, his eyes fixed on the yellow ball. As soon as Rascal mouthed the ball, David grabbed Rascal by his left front leg, pulling him closer until he had a tight grip on the little dog. After taking a quick glance around to be sure no one was watching, David threw Rascal into the back of his van and sped away hastily, ignoring the plaintiff whimpers from a very frightened Rascal.

We tailed the van as it weaved through the city, past the industrial park, to a small farm a few miles beyond the city. The van stopped in front of a red barn, and David snatched the quivering little dog from the back compartment. He entered the barn through a small doorway and greeted a big man in coveralls who was known by his childhood nickname, Butch. After exchanging a few words, Butch handed David a wad of bills and took Rascal under his arm. As the van scurried away, Rascal was dumped into a small cage at the back of the barn.

I looked askance at Albert, hoping he could shed some light on what had just happened. Albert was ready with his explanation: "The big man in the barn, Butch, is a breeder and trainer of fighting dogs— the ones that fight to the death with other dogs to the delight of the blood-thirsty crowds that frequent these events. Even though dog fighting is illegal in the U.S. and most other countries in the world, these laws are not able to stop this abhorrent practice that happens in this country on a regular basis."

"Why would Butch want a little dog like Rascal for the fights?" I wondered. "Surely he would be better off with a larger dog."

"Rascal will not be used for the fights," Albert continued, "he will be used as bait to train his fighting dogs, mainly American pit bull terriers. David, who is one of Butch's bait suppliers, hangs around the parks in the city hoping to snatch dogs that have wandered away from their owners. It is easy money for David, and he cares not a whit about what happens to the puppies after he sells them to Butch.

"An important aspect in the training of fighting dogs is to determine their 'gameness,' or desire to kill other animals. Not all pit bulls are naturally inclined to kill other dogs, but they can be trained to be killers at the hands of a skilled handler. This is where the bait comes in—they are used to encourage the killer instinct in the fighting dogs."

And then, much to my dismay, I got to witness the demise of poor little Rascal. It began with Butch pulling Rascal out of his cage and taping his little jaw shut with duct tape—to ensure he could not bite back. Butch dropped Rascal into his fighting pit, which was lined with sheets of plywood high enough to prevent any escape, and went to fetch Brutus, a one-year-old pit bull he was training for the dog fights. Brutus was a muscular specimen who was four or five times larger than Rascal. Brutus had started his training by killing rabbits, and now he would have the chance to kill another dog.

Butch gently lowered Brutus into the pit and immediately encouraged him to attack with his raucous chant of "kill, Brutus, kill." Brutus wasted no time in charging at little Rascal who was cowering in the corner. Rascal sensed Brutus would not be placated with a submissive pose, so he gamely darted away as Brutus lunged at him. Rascal was quicker and more agile than the pit bull, but he soon became exhausted. In the end, Brutus clamped his jaws on Rascal's little neck and crunched down. Rascal emitted several shrill yelps before his spine was crushed, killing him instantly. Brutus proudly paraded around the pit with Rascal hanging from his jaws, soaking up the praise from Butch, who was beaming with a lopsided grin.

As this horrific scene played out before my eyes, I felt a wave of nausea wash over me. My revulsion soon gave way to rage, and I wished I was present in physical form so I could tackle Butch and pin him to the ground until the police arrived.

"This is dreadful, Albert," I finally spit out my fury. "Why didn't you stop the grisly murder of this poor little dog?"

"I am not allowed to physically intervene to stop the appalling abuse you just witnessed or any of the other unspeakable crimes humans inflict on animals every day on your planet. And to make sure you get the message, I want to show you another example of egregious abuse that happens all too often on Earth."

Albert took my hand as we rose up through the morning sky and sped east toward the African continent. We swooped down onto a grassy savanna in Tanzania, landing next to a black rhinoceros female with her day-old calf. The mother was grazing peacefully on the tall grass while her baby wobbled behind on his unsteady legs. Soon the little guy snuggled up beside his mother, searching for her udder. His little tail flapped contentedly as he suckled the rich milk in big gulps.

This was the best part of his day—a chance to reconnect with the loving beast who had carried him in her womb for so many months.

It was a heart-warming scene that made me smile, thankful for the chance to see the magnificence of nature in a natural setting. There was nothing quite as glorious as the cycle of life on Earth and the enduring bond between a mother and her baby.

The peace was shattered suddenly with the crack of a high-powered rifle. The mother rhino dropped to her knees and rolled over, with blood spurting from a gaping hole in the side of her massive head. The baby hung close to her side, wondering why his mother had chosen to lay down before he had finished his meal.

Soon two poachers, with rifles slung over their shoulders, approached the fallen rhino and poked her to make sure she was dead. Then with big smiles plastered on their faces they cut off her horns with a small chainsaw and fled the scene in their Land Rover.

The baby rhino sensed something was wrong with his mama, but he didn't know what to do. He rested his little head on her neck, hoping she would get better soon because he was still hungry. As darkness crept up on the savanna, the little rhino snuggled closer to his mother in search of her udder, but he couldn't reach it. His plaintiff whimpering brought a lump to my throat, and I wished I could reach out to comfort the little guy. I wondered what would happen to him, and I feared he might die a slow death from starvation.

My fears proved to be unfounded as a pack of hungry hyenas slinked onto the scene looking for an easy meal. They jumped on the little rhino and began tearing chunks of flesh from his body in a blood-splattered frenzy. The baby tried to shake them off, except he was no match for the hungry pack and soon his little chest heaved for the last time.

Albert could see I was upset at what had transpired, so he tried his best to put a positive spin on this grisly scene.

"As cruel as it may seem, it was better for the little rhino to die quickly this way than to perish slowly from starvation. You cannot fault the hyenas—they did what nature intended for them in order to survive and feed their own young. The real culprits here are the poachers who shot the mother for her horns.

"I brought you here to show you how the dark side of humans can be activated by the lure of money. The poachers did not see their actions as a heinous crime against nature because they were blinded by their greed. The rhino horns they took with them would be smuggled out of the country and sold in China or Vietnam for $100,000 a kilogram, which is more than the price of gold. The only sure way to stop the poachers is to take away the market for the rhino horns, which is not an easy task. The people who buy the horns grind them into a powder and sell it for medicinal purposes to delusional customers who believe it can aid in the treatment of fever, liver ailments, hangovers, and even cancer. These medicinal claims, however, are entirely without merit because there is nothing in a rhino horn but keratin, which is the same protein found in human hair and nails. So ingesting rhino horn powder will produce no better results than swallowing chopped-up fingernails.

"As long as the myth about its therapeutic qualities persists, the black market in rhino horns will continue. The black rhinos you saw today are a critically endangered species primarily due to poaching. If humans can't find a way to stop the poachers, these magnificent creatures may disappear from the face of the Earth. And this would be another shameful scar on your race, which does not need to add another item to its long list of crimes against Mother Nature."

"Amen, Albert. I totally agree with your assessment. What can we do save the rhinos, the elephants, and all the other creatures who are slaughtered every year by men driven by greed?"

"You must do your best to ensure your fellow humans understand the significance of what is happening to God's creatures on your planet. This carnage will stop once your race fully comprehends the glorious majesty of the cycle of life on this planet and realizes that all animals, not just humans, have a right to share in the wonderful bounty provided by Mother Earth.

"The visits with the dog-fighting trainer and the rhino poaching here in Africa were designed to shock you—to hit you over the head with a two-by-four—in order to jolt you out of your comfortable stupor and spur you into action. Only you and your fellow humans living on the Earth plane can stop the gruesome maltreatment of the animals who share your planet. Passing laws to prevent dog fighting, poaching for ivory, shark fining, and all the other forms of animal cruelty is a good first step, but it has not stopped the abuse. What is needed is a seismic shift in attitude for those humans who regard your creatures as 'dumb animals' without intelligence, feelings, or souls. This segment of your civilization believes animals were put on your planet solely for the pleasure of humans, to be used or abused as they see fit. To humans with this mindset it is perfectly acceptable to beat, starve, torture, and kill Earth's creatures because they do not really count in the grand scheme of things.

"And it is not only the egregious acts of cruelty, like dog fighting, that are the problem. Every day somewhere on your planet you will find humans who will kick, punch, starve, or strangle their dogs and cats, mistreat their livestock, or hunt birds and other wild game just for the sport of it.

"It is not good enough for all the right-minded people to be content because they do not participate in such cruelty. They must be proactive and work diligently to ensure all humans understand that the creatures who share your planet were created by the Source and are connected to humans and to everything else in the universe, just like you. The villains who perpetrate these heinous crimes, and those who support their activities by attending dog fights, buying poached horns, or eating shark-fin soup, must be told in no uncertain terms by family, friends, neighbors, and the media that such conduct will no longer be tolerated. You must be vocal with your views, use gentle persuasion when appropriate, and always lead by example. The carnage can be stopped with a focused and persistent effort on the part of everyone who abhors animal cruelty.

"When you go back to your home do not forget what you saw here today. Keep it in the forefront of your mind and tell your story to everyone who will listen. One day your race will see the light, although you have a long way to go."

I felt like a student who had been scolded by the principal. But everything Albert said was right on the money. It seemed like it was a long uphill climb to persuade all humans to see the light, and then I remembered an old Chinese adage that every journey of a thousand miles begins with the first step.

"I have seen a lot on this trip, Albert, and I want to go home now to digest all the information you tossed my way."

"I will take you home, but I will be back soon. I have much more to show you, as we have only just begun."

Albert escorted me back to my bedroom and I slide back into my corporeal body, which was still asleep in my bed. The next morning I woke with a start as I remembered clearly everything I had seen with

Albert. I reached over and hugged my little dog, thankful she was safe and sound on my bed and fervently hoping she would never meet up with anyone like Butch.

I was happy to be back on familiar territory. My last trip with Albert was very disturbing, and I did not relish the thought of viewing any more scenes of abuse. Albert said he would return soon, but I didn't know whether to cheer him on or hide under my bed. Albert had an agenda for me, and I had no choice but to follow him whenever he next appeared regardless of the consequences.

When I took my miniature schnauzer for her morning walk, the memories of my last trip with Albert still smoldered in my mind. My thoughts were interrupted suddenly when an elderly lady stopped in front of us and exclaimed: "My God, you look just like your dog. Did you do this deliberately?"

I didn't know what to say, but I looked in the mirror when I got home to see what she meant. Sure enough, I had salt-and-pepper hair, a gray mustache, and a pot belly, just like Abby. *Oh well, if the shoe fits ...*

Albert came back that very same night and led me to our usual perch high above Earth. His face was inscrutable as he appeared to be deep in thought. I waited patiently for his next move while admiring the scene below. At long last Albert broke the silence.

"I think it is time for you to meet someone who plays a very important role in your life and the lives of all the other creatures on your planet."

Chapter Four
Gaia Speaks

I never failed to be overwhelmed by the beauty of my planet as it rotated slowly beneath my feet. The deep blue oceans were accented by the polar ice caps glittering in the bright sunlight and mottled by the darker hues of the land masses. White clouds dotted the northern hemisphere in fluffy clumps, leaving shadowy trails on the surface below. Planet Earth was something to behold—a precious gem floating in the blackness of space.

If all humans could see Earth from this perspective it would engender a major shift in attitude about the planet we inhabit. As soon as humankind truly understands its intimate connection to our planet, the abuse we heap on it every day would cease—ushering in a new era of love and respect for Mother Earth.

On some of my previous astral excursions with Albert I saw many examples of the horrendous pollution generated by humans that fouls our air, poisons our water, and kills our wildlife. I had implored Albert to tell me what I could do to help stop this abuse, but so far he had demurred. And so once again I raised the issue with Albert.

"I live on a beautiful, vibrant planet, Albert, which is in danger of becoming nothing more than a noxious garbage dump. What can I do to encourage my fellow humans to stop abusing Mother Earth with their pollution?"

"You must have been reading my mind, because the person you will meet next will provide you with plenty of ammunition. You have no doubt heard people refer to Mother Earth as though she was a living person, even though everyone thinks it is just a metaphor; however, there is more truth to this than you could ever imagine. Come with me and I will introduce you to Mother Earth. After that, you must do your best to disseminate her message around the world for all to hear.

"Humans must undergo a radical transformation of consciousness, and this movement must spring forth from the grass roots of your civilization. Once the masses have signed on to the change, the upper echelons of society will be forced to comply with the will of the people."

Albert motioned for me to follow him down through the clouds until we were hovering over the ice-covered northern pole. He clutched my arm and guided me downward until we had plunged beneath the icy waters of the Arctic Ocean, continuing our descent through the seabed until we came to a large underground cavern. The grotto was illuminated with a soft light that seemed to emanate from the walls without any obvious source. The floor of the cave was covered with glistening white stalagmites that pointed up at the slick, dripping stalactites hanging from the ceiling. I wondered why Albert had brought me to this underground chamber under the North Pole.

"Greetings, Gaia," Albert said at last to no one in particular, since he and I were the only ones in the cavern. "As promised, I brought my messenger with me. He has agreed to disseminate your message to all humankind."

I peered around the cave trying to see who Albert was addressing, but I could not detect anyone else. I was beginning to wonder if Albert had lost his marbles, until a gentle voice responded: "Greetings to you, Albert and Garnet. Thank you for meeting with me today. I have a lot of pent-up concerns, so bear with me as I vent all my frustrations.

"I am Gaia, known to some of you as Mother Earth. I am a living entity comprised of all that the planet Earth entails. I am the oceans, lakes, and rivers, the rocks and soil, and the mountain peaks, which form the outer shell of this planet, as well as everything beneath the surface right down to its molten core. I am the sum total of everything in and on this planet.

"It may surprise you, Garnet, to hear I am a living entity with feelings and emotions, but this is because your human senses are not able to detect my subtle existence. You think I am nothing more than a collection of inert molecules with none of the characteristics you typically associate with life. This springs from the very narrow view of life held by most humans—an attitude that will change as you expand your consciousness.

"While I understand your narrow definition of life derives from your current sensory limitations, I am appalled by the abuse humans have inflicted on me, the planet that provides a home for your race. Do you not understand you must live with the consequences of the damage you cause to your environment?

"I am wounded every day by the toxic chemicals humans spill into my rivers and the garbage you dump in my oceans. You slash and burn my magnificent forests to make way for your settlements, and your chemical emissions poison my atmosphere—which is the air you and my other creatures must breathe in order to survive. Your race extracts hydrocarbons from my bowels and then carelessly allows it to spill onto my fields and contaminate my waterways as the result of a ruptured pipeline or a hole in a tanker ship. Your pollution is not only a blight on the pristine beauty of Gaia, but it also causes unmitigated harm to the other creatures who share this planet.

"It wasn't always this way. For millions of years the human race lived in peaceful coexistence with Mother Earth and all of her creatures. During those golden years you lived close to nature and understood your home was like a sacred shrine—a place to be worshiped as the womb of all life. In those days humans shared a sense of oneness with Gaia—a unity that garnered mutual love and respect for all.

"And then it all began to change. At first the transition was almost unnoticeable, a slowly creeping deviation from the historic norm as your race developed new techniques to increase productivity and make life easier. The change accelerated at a geometric pace with the advent of the industrial revolution, and the situation has deteriorated ever since. Humans have become an invasive species, like a noxious weed that spreads its tentacles in every direction, smothering all life in its path.

"It is disheartening for me to watch this happen, not only for my sake but for all my other creatures who ask only for the opportunity to have a peaceful existence free from human interference. It is unconscionable for humans, prodded by their unbridled arrogance, to stomp on other creatures as though they are insignificant pawns in the conquest of this planet. All of my creatures have their own place in the universe, and their right to live on Earth must never be usurped by mankind.

"The solution to this problem requires humans to discard their fear and embrace love for Gaia and all of her creatures. Humans must expand their consciousness so they can move up the ladder of spiritual enlightenment. Only then will we all be able to live together in peace and harmony.

"I am optimistic this can be achieved, although I am frustrated at the glacial pace of the change. So I have begun my own campaign to spur you into action. I have many arrows in my quiver, and I will use them if necessary to awaken you from your stupor. You may have noticed a recent increase in weather phenomena that is much more extreme and intense than normal. This is because I have unleashed more devastating hurricanes, tornados, and floods than ever before, while the pace and severity of earthquakes and volcanic eruptions around the world has increased. This is just a warning shot across your bow. What your scientists attribute to climate change is really Gaia fighting back. And make no mistake about it—I am quite capable of causing terrible havoc to your civilization if I so choose.

"I do not wish to cause unnecessary harm to your people. I only want to preserve this planet as a sacred and inviolable home for all of my flora and fauna, including humans. I beseech you to change your ways so you can enjoy life in harmony with a new Earth that will be free from violence and abuse. Modify your behavior, humans, or suffer the consequences. The choice is yours."

I stood there in silence, chastised by the onslaught from Gaia and embarrassed to be a member of the human race. I did not know how to respond because so much of what she said rang true. I could only slink off with my tail between my legs, beaten and despondent.

I followed Albert out of the cavern and back to our lofty perch high above my planet. This was a call to action, for sure, and I hoped I could somehow rally the troops to avoid disaster.

"I am heartened to see you have gained some new insights about your planet from Gaia," Albert said at last. "But you should know she did not reveal all of her secrets. There is more to Gaia than you could ever imagine, and I will show you a couple of her hidden gems to give you a better understanding of the complex world of Mother Earth."

Chapter Five
Gentle Giants

We headed toward the North American continent, floating down through the clouds and into the dense forests and mountains of the Pacific Northwest. In the darkness of the night we touched down in a small meadow dotted with wildflowers.

"Why did you bring me here, Albert?"

"I want you to meet an interesting life form on your planet— intelligent creatures who have coexisted with humans for millions of years without any open contact with your species. They have been the stuff of legends for centuries, often called Sasquatch, Bigfoot, or Yeti. These creatures have a highly developed sense of perception and can communicate by telepathy, which is why they will be able to see and hear us in astral form."

I heard a rustling in the thick bush at the far edge of the meadow, and then a large humanoid creature emerged and stood in front of us, bathed in the moonlight. She was about nine feet tall as she stood upright on her legs, with long arms hanging down to her knees. She had a big ape-like head with large round eyes that stared at us intently. Her body was covered with thick dark-brown hair that glistened softly in the pale light from the moon. We stared at each other for several minutes until Albert broke the silence.

"Greetings, Zana. As we discussed before, I brought a human in astral form to meet you. His name is Garnet, and he will have many questions for you."

"Welcome, Albert and Garnet. What would you like to know?" Zana responded telepathically.

"What kind of creature are you, and where did you come from?" I began.

"My species originated millions of years ago in the African continent. We were the result of an experiment conducted by a race of humanoid extraterrestrials that visited Earth frequently from their

25

home planet near the center of our galaxy. They artificially inseminated Gigantopithecus females (which are now extinct primates) with their sperm to create a tall humanoid creature with an extra-large brain and enhanced sensory perception. This was the origin of our species, and my people eventually spread throughout Europe and Asia and then to North America via the Bering land bridge.

"We live on all of your continents, except Antarctica, in a peaceful coexistence with Mother Earth and all of her creatures. We eat leaves, twigs, roots, and berries, and we do not eat animal flesh or kill other creatures. We have coexisted with humans for millions of years, although we chose not to have open contact with your species. We find humans to be too aggressive and violent for our liking, so we avoid any interaction with them.

"Our enhanced perception allows us to communicate with one another telepathically, and this allows us to silently warn others about approaching humans. We also have the sensory capacity to detect, and distinguish, other creatures for miles around—kind of like an animal-sensitive radar system. This allows us to spot and avoid any humans in our vicinity. We are nocturnal creatures with highly developed night vision, and during the daylight hours we live in our underground caves with carefully concealed entrances. All of these factors have allowed us to avoid open contact with humans.

"On rare occasions some of my people have been careless—leaving behind footprints or allowing humans to spot them from afar. But generally we have been very adept at avoiding detection by humans, which becomes more difficult every year as your civilization continues to encroach on our traditional territory. We all dread the day when the truth about us becomes public knowledge to humans."

"You seem to be very intelligent," I concluded. "Why did you not develop any technology?"

"We decided eons ago to eschew technology in favor of living simply and close to nature. We wanted to live in harmony with our planet and all of its flora and fauna, and we feared technology would lead us down the same path that humans were following. We watched your civilization develop its technology over the years, and we concluded that your technological advances fostered materialism and aggression and encouraged your unjustified sense of superiority over all other creatures on this planet. Human technology has created sophisticated weapons that are very effective at killing animals and other humans, and this has led to numerous wars and violent conflicts. And your weapons of mass destruction could destroy all life on Earth in the blink of an eye.

"Even if you do not destroy our planet with your weapons, you are slowly poisoning Earth with your pollution, which has increased exponentially in the last few decades.

"We are very concerned about the future of life on Earth, but we do not have any means to stop this inexorable death march. What we need is a seismic shift in human behavior—a new paradigm where human anger, hate, and violence are replaced by love and compassion for Mother Earth and all of her creatures. We can only hope this will happen before we all perish."

"Have you thought about taking your message directly to humans?" I asked.

"We did consider this approach, but decided it was unworkable. We do not have a verbal language and humans have not yet learned how to utilize more of their brain capacity to communicate telepathically. So we feared humans would treat us as dumb animals that should be put on display in your zoos. We would rather die than live in a cage."

I did not know what to say. Zana had hit the nail on the head for the most part. I was embarrassed to acknowledge the current state of human civilization, which this gentle giant had described with heartfelt eloquence.

"I echo your concerns, Zana; however, there is a ray of hope beaming through the stormy clouds. Every day more and more humans are embracing spiritual enlightenment and discarding their negative emotions. I sincerely hope this movement will someday change the course of human destiny before it is too late.

"Thank you for meeting with me today, Zana. I will do my best to tell your story to my fellow humans, although it is likely no one will believe me without physical proof of your existence. Farewell for now."

I gave Zana an astral hug, and then watched as she disappeared silently into a dense thicket of trees. Albert tugged at my arm, and I followed him back to my home. Before he left, I pumped him for more information about Gaia and her untold secrets, but he demurred. He told me I should take some time to assimilate what I had just seen, and he would return soon to take me on a trek to the Emerald Isle where I would meet an emissary from a civilization of little people that has secretly inhabited Earth for many centuries.

Chapter Six
Little People

As I waited for Albert to return, I looked back on my recent astral adventures trying to piece together what I had learned into a coherent paradigm. Before I met Albert, it was apparent to me our planet was inhabited by humans, plants, and animals, with humans being the dominant species and the only intelligent life form on our planet. But my astral excursions with Albert had opened my eyes to several hidden truths about our planet.

I now know all animals have souls, just like humans, and they all have feelings and emotions. Some of Earth's creatures, like dolphins and whales, have highly developed brains with intellects that surpass those of humans in many ways. I discovered they can communicate with one another, and with their cousins on another planet, by telepathy. They are more spiritually evolved than most humans as they understand their connection to Mother Earth and all of her creatures. They are dismayed by the abuse they have received over the years from humans, and do not understand why humans are unable to control their negative emotions, which fosters conflicts and wars among humans, the killing and maiming of animals, and the pollution of our planet.

And on my last trip with Albert I met with a member of a secretive race of intelligent humanoids known as the Sasquatch, who regard humans as a violent and aggressive race that rules the world with a reckless disregard for the welfare of Mother Earth and her other creatures.

This was the picture I had so far, although I wondered if there were more pieces to the puzzle about Mother Earth and her inhabitants. I was anxious to meet with the little people, as Albert had promised, and I was beginning to think this was just the tip of the iceberg.

So when Albert made his appearance once again, I jumped in with my questions.

"I am curious about the planet I live on, Albert, and I would like to know if there are any other surprises about life on Earth you have not yet revealed to me. Human history is replete with legends of mythical creatures that roamed our planet in years gone by. I am talking about unicorns, minotaurs, elves, fairies, werewolves, vampires, and the like. And then there are the fabled creatures from present day that have been spotted by humans but never captured, like the Loch Ness Monster and Ogopogo. Is there any truth to these legends?"

"As Shakespeare said in *Hamlet*, there are more things in heaven and earth than are dreamt of in your philosophy. Most legends have some basis in reality although the stories are often embellished as they are passed down from generation to generation. Earth is populated with many creatures that humans have not yet discovered or whose existence is generally denied. It is not important at this time for you to learn more about these fables, because you have more pressing matters to attend to. But as promised, I will take you to meet one of the mythical spirits in Ireland, commonly known as fairies."

I was excited about the prospect of going to Ireland, the land of my maternal ancestors. When I was a young child my mother would pin a green shamrock to my shirt every year on St. Patrick's Day, which I promptly removed as soon as I got on the school bus. When I was in college I finally learned to appreciate the benefits of St. Patrick's Day— being able to drink green beer at the local pub. My Irish relatives were a happy and lively bunch who worked hard and enjoyed family gatherings where everyone could tap their feet in time to the merry Irish music.

I followed Albert down through the wispy cirrus clouds until we landed in a small glen in the rolling countryside. We strolled beside a burbling brook of pellucid water that sparkled in the sunlight. The lush green grass beside the little stream beckoned me to lie down in its verdant embrace and gaze up at the clouds as they morphed whimsically from shape to shape. The morning sun bathed me in its warm glow and the refreshing breeze gently caressed my ethereal body.

What a wonderful place for a picnic, I thought. All I needed was a hot shepherd's pie and a cold Guinness to wash it down. What more could I possibly want? But I knew my taskmaster had not brought me here to have fun, so I sat down beside him on a large boulder near the stream, waiting for something to happen.

Before long I noticed movement out of the corner of my eye, coming from behind a clump of trees. When I glanced in that direction I could see nothing unusual, but Albert walked up to the bush and disappeared behind the foliage. Moments later he emerged holding the hand of a little person who stepped gingerly at his side. The little one looked like a tiny human, no more than three feet tall, with an exquisite face peeking out from a fringe of golden curls that cascaded down to her shoulders. Her sparkling green eyes harmonized perfectly with her forest-green frock, which was blazoned with tiny emeralds. She looked like a tiny perfect china doll.

"I would like you to meet Breena. She is a fairy, one of the fabled sprites of Ireland," Albert proudly announced.

I stood up and bowed, not knowing for sure how to greet a fairy. Breena smiled and held out her hand, which I grasped gently in mine. Her skin was soft and smooth, like a baby's cheek, and her grip was delicate. I stared into her eyes, enchanted by her beauty, until Albert broke the silence.

"You had asked me if there was any truth to the legends about the wee folk of Ireland. Breena stands before you today as living proof of the existence of fairies. Would you like to ask her any questions?"

Where should I begin? I thought. Breena was an intriguing little person, and I was bursting with questions. "Can you tell me about yourself and the other fairies, Breena? Where do you live and how do you manage to avoid detection by humans?"

"We have been living on this land and the neighboring islands for eons. Before humans arrived we had an idyllic existence. We lived in peaceful harmony with Mother Nature and all her creatures, and we never fought or squabbled among ourselves. Injuring another fairy was unthinkable to us, as we understood our connection to each other and to the Source. We lived close to the land—growing vegetables and fruit and raising goats for their milk. We did not consume animal flesh and we treated all creatures with dignity and respect.

"Our modest needs were easily filled, which allowed us to spend most of our time singing and playing games. We loved to frolic in the forests and glens, dance to the merry tunes from our fiddlers, and laugh at the antics of our children. We had no fears or apprehensions about anything, and everyone enjoyed a happy and carefree life.

"And then our world was turned upside down when humans arrived on our peaceful little island. At first we welcomed them with open arms thinking they were just like us, only taller. We soon learned, much to our chagrin, that humans were very different from us. They were aggressive and violent creatures who fought among themselves and took what they wanted from the land without any regard for us or the other animals in our world. They hunted and slaughtered the creatures of this island with ruthless abandon, and they tried to enslave us to do their bidding.

"Fortunately for us, our wise leaders foresaw the looming danger, and they acted quickly to save us from disaster. They sent out a plea for help to the angels who watched over our people, and these special spirits aided our escape from the cruel clutches of the humans. They helped us build underground cities with carefully concealed entrances, and they showed us how to tap into the energy of the universe to make ourselves invisible to humans when needed. They taught us how to manipulate matter and move objects with the power of thought.

"And so we have lived in our underground cities ever since. We are still happy and carefree, but we do miss the sunshine and the rain, the green grass and leafy trees, and the other creatures of our land. Because it is against our nature to be violent we have never tried to rid our island of humans. Instead, we take turns making discreet jaunts to the surface to dance in the sunlight and breathe in the fresh salt air."

"The humans on this island have many legends about wee folk and fairies. How was it possible for them to see fairies when you live underground and have the ability to render yourselves invisible?" I asked Breena.

"Fairies have been spotted from time to time when some of us have been careless," Breena responded, "and on other occasions we have allowed ourselves to be seen in order to help humans who have already rejected the dark side of humanity. Our ability to move objects telekinetically allows us to perform 'magic' in the eyes of these humans. And sometimes our mischievous fairies will pull harmless pranks on humans to get a few laughs, although we generally discourage these hijinks."

"Is there anything I can do to help you and your people?" I wondered.

"You can follow Albert's advice and share his wisdom with your race. With a lot of concerted effort it will be possible one day for humans to discard their violent ways and embrace love and compassion for Mother Earth and all of her inhabitants. When this happens, we will be able to return to the surface of our beautiful island to live in peaceful coexistence with your people."

"Thank you, Breena, for sharing your story. I am saddened by the plight of your people who must live underground to avoid humans. I can see that fairies are resilient little people who have resolved to live as best they can in the face of adversity. I will tell your story to all who will listen, and hopefully one day you can come out of hiding and once again dance openly in sunlight. Farewell for now."

I gave little Breena a tender hug and watched her disappear into the thicket of trees. Albert motioned it was time to leave, and we floated up through the white clouds, leaving Ireland far behind. Albert had satisfied my curiosity about fairies, but my visit with Breena had left me feeling sad and despondent about the state of my planet. Albert could sense my sullen mood, so he wrapped his arm around my shoulders, promising to show me something positive and uplifting on our next trip. *Good news at last*, I thought. *I can hardly wait.*

Chapter Seven

Milk of Human Kindness

I have often wondered if there is any real hope for humankind. The nightly news is filled with reports of violence: murders, kidnappings, terrorist bombs, and armed conflicts. It seems as though humans are incapable of setting aside their differences and treating everyone with dignity and respect. In *Dancing Forever with Spirit*, the Council of Wise Ones told me we were getting help from our extraterrestrial friends and from an influx of advanced souls who have recently incarnated on Earth, and they were confident humanity would turn the corner before it was too late. But some days I was overwhelmed with skepticism, leaving me restless and dispirited when I thought about the future of my planet.

The next time Albert made one of his nightly appearances, I let him know what was on my mind.

"I am feeling a little depressed about the current state of human affairs," I began. "It seems we are more violent and aggressive than ever before. Instead of advancing up the ladder of spiritual enlightenment, we seem to take one step forward and two steps back. We are supposed to be renouncing our negative emotions and increasing our vibratory rates, but too many of us are backsliding toward a world filled with anger, hate, and violence. I don't know if we can turn this around before we destroy ourselves and everything else on this planet."

"Keep your chin up, my friend," Albert replied. "Things are actually much better than you think. The problem with your news media is they tend to sensationalize their newscasts to attract viewers and increase their market share. They think people are more inclined to listen to stories about tragedies and violence than stories about human kindness. This is why they focus on shootings, sexual assaults, and terrorist attacks. The volunteers who work tirelessly to help downtrodden people around the world who are sick, injured, or starving do not warrant news coverage because it is too mundane. Hence your perception of what is happening, which you glean from newspapers and TV news, is distorted.

"I promised to do something on our next trip that would cheer you up, so let me show you a few things that are happening right now on your planet that will restore your faith in humanity."

I trailed Albert as he headed toward West Africa, where we glided to a halt in the small city of Kailuhan, in Sierra Leone. Albert explained that a major Ebola outbreak that had started in Guinea, killing many people, had spread to neighboring countries, including Sierra Leone. Ebola was a very dangerous virus for which there was no cure and no vaccine. The fatality rate for those who were infected with this disease was around 90 percent.

We were standing near an Ebola treatment center built by Médecins Sans Frontières (MSF), also known as Doctors Without Borders, which held dozens of Ebola-infected patients on hospital cots housed in a collection of tents. They all suffered from the classic symptoms of this virus: headaches, fever, muscle aches, vomiting, and diarrhea.

Volunteer doctors and nurses, wearing full protective gear, did their best to alleviate the symptoms and keep the patients as comfortable as possible. These MSF volunteers came from many different nations and were all dedicated health professionals. They worked long days under grueling conditions without compensation—except for the satisfaction of knowing they were helping other humans in desperate need of medical attention.

We zeroed in on one of the cots that held an eight-month-old infant who had a high fever and painful muscle aches. Her mother had passed away two days before from this horrible disease, and the baby was all alone except for a doctor who was gently sponging her with a damp cloth.

Albert noted that the doctor, Jessica, had been working at the treatment center for several weeks along with her fiancé, Christopher. They were both graduates of the Stanford School of Medicine where they first met and fell in love. Their romance had continued when they were both accepted for the Internal Medicine residency program at Georgetown University Medical Center. When they completed this program, they jointly decided to hold off pursuing lucrative medical careers and starting a family in favor of volunteering for a year with Doctors Without Borders.

The infant Jessica was sponging suddenly threw up, spewing green vomit all over herself. Jessica carefully cleaned the infant and continued with the sponge bath. Then the little tyke began to whimper softly, longing for her mother, and Jessica could hold out no longer. She scooped up the baby and cuddled her warmly to her bosom while singing the lullaby her mother sang to her years ago. Jessica's eyes welled up with tears as she gently swayed the infant, hoping to rock her to sleep. When the baby girl stopped whimpering, Jessica lay her down on the cot, only then realizing the infant had quietly passed on—comforted by the warm embrace of this kind and loving doctor. Jessica covered the little body with a sheet and said a silent prayer for God to take care of this special little human who had such a brief and tragic life.

I watched all of this with a lump in my throat, feeling sorry for the baby, but knowing that her soul was transitioning to the Spirit Side where she would be greeted by her mother. I was thankful Albert had brought me here today, and I now understood what he was trying to tell me—that human love and compassion is everywhere around us, although we do not always notice the goodness in other humans.

I followed Albert up into the evening sky, heading west toward a bustling city in New England, not far from the Atlantic coast. We landed in a downtrodden area of the city, its streets lined with dilapidated wooden houses and slum apartment buildings. I noticed a young man in his mid-twenties walking dejectedly down the street. He was wearing blue jeans and a T-shirt, and his face was covered with a short scraggly beard.

Albert told me the young man, Eddy, had been laid off a few weeks before when the small manufacturing firm he had worked for went out of business. Eddy was an orphan who had lost his parents and younger brother in a tragic house fire when he was only five. As he had no relatives who were willing to take him in, he had been placed in a foster home. Eddy lived in three different foster homes over the years until he fled the last one when he was sixteen. His last foster father had been physically abusive, and Eddy had grown weary of the weekly beatings he got for no good reason.

Eddy never finished high school, and he had no trade skills. He had drifted from job to job in the construction industry, earning only enough to scrape by. Three years ago his luck had changed when he found steady work with a company that built small utility trailers. Eddy was mechanically inclined, and he took pride in assembling the trailers. The husband and wife team who owned the plant were kind and generous to their employees, and Eddy couldn't have been any happier.

And then disaster struck. The warehouse where the trailers were assembled caught fire one night and burned to the ground. As the owners did not have enough insurance money to rebuild, they had to cease operations and lay off all employees.

Since then Eddy had been pounding the pavement looking for work. He had just pulled the last of his cash from his bank account, and he had no idea how he would be able to come up with the rent money for his small apartment when it was due in two weeks.

We watched Eddy wander down the street, his ruddy face lined with sadness. After a few blocks Eddy stopped suddenly in front of a middle-aged woman who was sitting on the sidewalk, sobbing softly. She looked like a homeless street person, with ragged and torn jeans and a dirty jacket. Her hair was greasy and stringy, and it looked like she hadn't had a bath in weeks.

There was something about this person that tugged at Eddy's heartstrings, and he knelt down to peer into her rheumy gray eyes. He saw loneliness and desperation, and her eyes pleaded silently for help. On impulse, Eddy gently pulled the woman to her feet and helped her limp into a nearby diner. He ordered her a hearty breakfast of bacon, eggs, and pancakes, along with a pot of hot coffee. The street lady wolfed down her breakfast without saying a word, as Eddy watched in silence. When she finished she stood up, gave Eddy a warm hug, and whispered, "Thank you, kind sir" in a trembling voice.

Eddy followed her out of the diner and reached into his pocket to retrieve the last of his cash, a ten-dollar bill and fifty-five cents in change. With a wink and a smile he handed her the money and continued his trek down the street. Even though he had given away the last of his cash, Eddy now had a bounce in his step and his smile lit up his whole face.

We tailed Eddy back to his apartment building where he retrieved his mail from the mailbox in the foyer. As he sorted through the bills he noticed an envelope with a return address he did not recognize. Eddy reluctantly opened the envelope, hoping it was not another notice from a collection agency. His heart began to thump wildly in his chest as he read the letter. It was from a law firm advising that his estranged uncle Henry, whom Eddy had not heard from since the death of his family, had passed away, leaving his estate to his only surviving relative. Enclosed with the letter was a check made out to Eddy in the amount of $54,245.

Eddy danced around his apartment in a frenzy of joy, his heart filled with hope for a new beginning. He flopped down on his couch and looked up at the ceiling, mouthing a silent prayer of gratitude, as tears streamed down his beaming face. He ran out of his apartment and down the street to where he had last seen the homeless woman, but she was nowhere to be seen anywhere in a three-block radius. Eddy gave up the search and marched to his bank where he handed his check to the clerk, his hand trembling with excitement. Moments later, Eddy left the bank shouting, "Hallelujah" as loudly as he could, not caring a whit about the stares he got from the bystanders. He skipped down the street toward his apartment, eager to begin the next chapter of his life.

A tear came to my eye as I watched Eddy disappear around the corner. I looked over at Albert, who was watching me intently.

"Was the homeless woman a special soul sent to help Eddy?" I asked Albert.

"All souls are special in their own unique ways," Albert replied. "And all humans on your planet have the capacity to spread kindness and compassion to everyone around them. Someday Eddy will meet this street person on the other side of the veil, and the reunion will be heartwarming."

"You know, Albert, the homeless lady we just saw with Eddy reminds me of the first time I met you. You looked a lot like this homeless lady, except you smelled much worse. But unlike Eddy, I did not get a check in the mail after I met you."

"True, but you got something much more valuable—the opportunity to hang out with someone who is wise, charming, charismatic, and very witty, not to mention incredibly good looking. Most people would give anything for that opportunity."

"It sounds wonderful, Albert, when do I get to meet this person?"

"Very funny. Forgive me if I don't convulse in a spasm of belly laughter."

Albert turned abruptly and rose up into the sky, and I hurried to catch up. We stopped at our usual perch high above Earth where we watched the sun set over the West Coast of North America. I loved to admire the breathtaking beauty of the blue orb below us—a scene that sent shivers down my spine every time I viewed my home planet from space.

A gentle tug on my arm signaled it was time to go, and Albert guided me down toward southern California. We landed on the front lawn of a nice two-story house nestled in a cul-de-sac lined with houses that looked much the same. It looked like a typical middle-class suburb, with all the houses featuring double-attached garages and clay-tile roofs. All was quiet, except for a late-model Mustang that motored down the street and parked on the driveway of the house next to us.

Albert revealed that the young man, Tim, was living at home with his parents while attending college. He had spent the evening with his girlfriend, Jennifer, and was now anxious to get some shut-eye before his alarm went off to wake him for another day of classes. Tim was in one of life's sweet spots: he enjoyed the classes in the accounting program he was taking at college and he was in love with Jennifer. He looked forward to finishing his degree, finding a job, and marrying his sweetheart.

Tim was heading toward the front door of his house when something made him stop and look at the house on his left. He noticed what looked like flames flickering in the basement window. When he moved closer for a better view, he could see a fire in the basement. Tim quickly called 911 to report the blaze and then tried to enter through the front door to warn the people inside. Tim recalled that the husband and wife had left the day before for a short vacation, leaving their three young children with their grandmother.

The front door was locked, so Tim held his finger on the doorbell button while pounding loudly on the wooden door. After what seemed like an eternity, Tim heard the deadbolt retract and the door opened. Smoke billowed out the doorway as the grandmother, who was clutching the ten-month-old baby girl and her three-year-old brother, stumbled out of the house. She staggered and nearly fell on the step, but Tim caught her and helped them to safety on his front lawn.

The grandmother was nearly overcome by the smoke, but she managed to croak to Tim that the third child, a five-year-old girl, was still in the house because she was not able to carry all three of them at one time.

Without hesitation Tim bolted into the house and sprinted up the stairs. Smoke was swirling everywhere, which made it difficult for him to see. He found the little girl in one of the bedrooms, sound asleep in her bed. Tim scooped her into his arms and raced down the stairs, only to trip over a toy dump truck that had been left on the bottom step. He cradled the child as he fell and twisted his body to make sure she did not hit the floor. He hit the slate tile in the foyer with a thump but managed to hang on to his precious package. The smoke stung his eyes and his lungs ached, while scenes from his life flashed before his eyes. But Tim was a fighter, and he slowly got to his feet and stumbled down the front step. By this time the firefighters had arrived, and they carried Tim and the little girl to the waiting ambulance where the paramedics administered oxygen to both of them before speeding away to the hospital.

I watched the house go up in flames as the firefighters hosed down the houses on either side to keep them safe. The grandmother and the two children she had rescued were suffering from smoke inhalation, but they were discharged from the hospital the next morning.

We followed Tim's ambulance to the hospital where he and his little neighbor were treated for severe smoke inhalation. Fortunately, the prognosis was good for both of them, although they would have to remain in the hospital for several days. Early the next morning, Tim's parents and Jennifer were sitting by his bed when he woke up. Jennifer threw her arms around him and exclaimed: "You are my brave hero, Tim."

Tim cracked a big smile and replied: "I am not a hero. I am just an ordinary guy who did what anyone else would have done in the same situation. I happened to be in the right place at the right time, and I did what I had to do. Thank God it turned out all right."

And I felt thankful Albert had brought me here to watch the milk of human kindness flowing freely. Albert clutched my elbow, and we rose up through the wispy white clouds to park ourselves once again high above my beautiful home planet, which floated like a precious jewel in the ocean of space.

Albert was right, I thought. Humans are indeed capable of compassionate acts of kindness to other people, including complete strangers. If only we could fan that spark of compassion we all have within us to kindle our innate desire to love and be loved, our world would be a much happier place. All of us, and the other creatures on our planet, would thrive in the joyful aftermath of our shift to a higher state of consciousness. Albert has shown us the path, but it is up to each of us to stride boldly toward that elusive goal of spiritual enlightenment.

I felt good about what I had seen today—it restored my faith in humankind. But I knew the dark side of humanity still lurked in the dusky corners of our society, and our world would not be free from strife until every last bit of hatred and violence had been eradicated from our planet. This was not an impossible goal to achieve, although it would not be an easy journey to get there. I guess that is why Earth is considered one of the toughest schools in the universe. Like they say, when the going gets tough, the tough get going. The time for action was upon us.

I asked Albert to take me home because I had a lot of things to sort out, and I wanted to get started. But I wanted to ask Albert a question before he left—something that had been troubling me for quite some time.

"You have shown me two sides of humanity: one is seamy and ugly, and the other is compassionate and uplifting. These two facets are constantly knocking heads as they strive for supremacy on this planet. You mentioned before that Earth has harbored many human civilizations in the past that did not survive, and I wonder if they perished because they could not control the dark side of humanity. Have humans always been this way?"

"Humans on Earth have not always had to struggle with the fear and violence that plague your society. One of your earlier civilizations that had conquered their negative emotions perished through no fault of their own as the result of a rare cosmological event in the history of your planet. When I come back I will let you view the Akashic Records to see the last days of this civilization that thrived eons ago before disappearing tragically. But for that unfortunate event, your civilization today might be much more pleasant and peaceful than what you have right now."

Chapter Eight
Eden on Earth

When Albert returned several nights later he took me back to the majestic Hall of Records in the white city of Aglaia. This building houses the Akashic Records, which stores the details of every life that has ever been lived anywhere in the universe. I had been here before with Albert (as described in *Dancing Forever with Spirit*), and I was eager to see what Albert would show me today.

We entered one of the viewing rooms with a large holographic globe floating in the center, filled with blue and white vapors that swirled in a random pattern. Albert waved his hand over the globe and the vapors gave way to a stunning vista. It looked like a tropical rain forest nestled beside a broad savanna lush with green grasses and shrubs. Near the edge of the forest was the smoldering peak of a large volcano rising above the trees.

In response to my puzzled expression, Albert described the setting for me: "This is Earth, about sixty-five million years ago, at the end of the Cretaceous period. We are looking at an area that is now in Central America. I want to show you the last days of the dinosaurs and the human civilization that lived at the same time."

The scene in the globe focused on the broad savanna, and soon I was viewing a landscape that reminded me of one of my favorite movies, *Jurassic Park*. I noticed a group of triceratops grazing peacefully on the lush vegetation. They were large and imposing, and I was excited to see an extinct species of dinosaur firsthand. A mile to the north of the triceratops was a herd of hadrosaurs nestled down for a nap in the hot afternoon sun. Then I noticed a rustle of activity in the tall grass nearby, and when the scene in the globe shifted for a close-up view I saw a dozen or so humans crouching down low as they snuck closer to the sleeping hadrosaurs. They were dressed in simple sleeveless tunics and sandals made from animal hides. Their skin was a golden bronze and their shiny black hair reached down to their shoulders. The group was half men and half women, and everyone carried a long spear tipped with a sharp metallic point.

It was obvious this was a hunting party, and I was captivated by the drama as it unfolded before my eyes. With practiced stealth the hunters crept closer to the nearest hadrosaur and then pounced on their prey, jabbing the slumbering animal repeatedly with their spears. The startled creature jumped to its feet as the rest of the herd scattered in a frenzy. But the targeted beast was surrounded by the hunting party, and the puncture wounds from the spears began to take their toll. It eventually stumbled and fell, and the end came quickly when one of the hunters severed its spine with a short sword.

The humans quickly skinned the hadrosaur and carved the meat into large chunks that were strung from poles with ropes made from vines. Each pole was hoisted to the shoulders of a pair of hunters, and the triumphant humans hastened off with the fruits of their labor. They headed toward a large walled city near the edge of the forest. As the scene zoomed in, I could see the sturdy walls, which completely encircled the city, were twenty feet tall, two feet thick, and constructed with stones and mortar. A large drawbridge-like door made of heavy timber planks blocked the main entrance.

The sentries on the top of the wall lowered the drawbridge for the hunting party, which broke into a lope when they heard a spine-chilling roar behind them. It came from a charging tyrannosaurus rex who was following the scent of their kill. I held my breath until the hunters had scrambled safely through the gate and the drawbridge was closed tight. The T. rex rammed his massive head repeatedly against the stout timbers, but they held fast. Eventually the furious predator turned away to find other prey.

When I was finally able to break away from the drama in the globe, I asked Albert for an explanation: "You mentioned this scene was from the Cretaceous period on Earth around sixty-five million years ago, even though most anthropologists maintain humans have been on Earth for only seven million years. How do you explain the presence of humans in the age of dinosaurs?"

Albert smiled as though he had been anticipating my question. "Your anthropologists are basing their conclusions on the evidence they have found so far about the origin of humans on your planet. They are not aware of this civilization because nothing remained of it after the cataclysm destroyed their city and annihilated most of the dinosaurs. In fact, there have been many human civilizations that once thrived on Earth that have not yet been discovered by your scientists.

"The humans in this walled city were seeded here by extraterrestrial beings (ETs) several thousand years before this point in time. This was the first attempt to introduce humans to your planet, and it worked wonderfully for a very long time. The humans who were planted here were allowed to develop on their own, without any interference from the ETs, and the Council of Wise Ones was very pleased with the unique characteristics of this society.

"Unlike human civilization in the twenty-first century, these early humans understood and practiced the principle of equality for all. Men and women were equal in all respects. They shared the responsibility for hunting and growing food, raising children, making clothes and weapons, and preparing meals. The tribal leaders, who were elected every three years by a general vote of the populace, alternated between men and women on a regular basis.

"They had no crime as the citizens clearly understood they were souls having a human journey on Earth. Because they knew they were intimately connected to each other and to everything else in the universe, they believed harming a fellow human was tantamount to harming themselves. Thus they were content to live by the Golden Rule.

"This society was primitive by your standards, but everyone worked for the common good and they enjoyed all the material wealth they needed or desired. They did not have any form of money and everyone lived in the same size of one-story shanty built from wood harvested from the forest. Relationships between men and women did not cause any discourse because of their unique philosophy: they understood that monogamous relationships could cause jealousy and foster violence, so they did not have the family units prevalent in your society. Men and women did not form lifelong partnerships; instead, every person had sexual liaisons with many different partners over the years. There was no possessiveness or jealousy, because no one had any special attachments to a member of the opposite sex.

"Mothers breast fed their babies for the first year, then turned them over to the women and men in charge of child-rearing, where they were raised and educated in a communal setting along with all the other children.

"These people lived in harmony with Mother Earth and all of her creatures. They did not pollute their environment, except for a small of amount of smoke from cooking and smelting fires, and they recycled all human and food waste in compost bins. They grew vegetables in their garden plots and foraged fruit from the forest. They only killed animals necessary for food and clothing and they used every part of the animal—nothing was wasted. And when one of them passed away, the body was left in the forest as a meal for the scavengers—their way of giving something back to nature.

"They never ventured very far from their city, and had no interest in exploring the outside world or starting new settlements. They kept their population in balance by ensuring new births would only replace the people who had passed away each year. They had discovered that eating the leaves of a certain plant that grew in the forest would prevent pregnancy, and they used this to regulate the number of babies born each year.

"Then one day their civilization vanished, along with most of the dinosaurs and many of the plant varieties that existed at the time. The end came swiftly and without any warning when an asteroid crashed down on the Yucatan Peninsula. The huge explosion sent tons of dust into the atmosphere and caused severe seismic shifts in the Earth's crust. This triggered numerous earthquakes and the eruption of hundreds of volcanoes around the world, including the one close to this human settlement. Within a very short period this idyllic city on the plain was deluged in a flood of molten lava that buried everything to a depth of several hundred meters. No one escaped this catastrophe, and no traces of this civilization remained when the smoke cleared.

"The dust and smoke spewed forth by the volcanoes, combined with the dust from the asteroid impact, totally blocked out the sun's rays for several years and resulted in a 'nuclear winter' that caused a severe drop in the temperature of the planet. This led to the extinction of most of the dinosaurs and many of the plants that had thrived for millions of years. I won't show you the end of this civilization because it would be too painful to watch. We can only speculate on how this society would have developed if the asteroid had missed the Earth."

"Why didn't the ETs step in to prevent this catastrophe?" I pondered.

"Because they were not allowed to directly interfere with the course of events on Earth. They had to watch helplessly as this disaster unfolded, knowing full well that they would no doubt try again to seed human life on Earth. Unlike other human civilizations that were destroyed through the reckless actions of their citizens, this one did nothing to contribute to its downfall. They perished from a random cosmic occurrence that could not have been predicted or prevented.

"Do not shed too many tears, because the souls of the humans who perished here have long since reincarnated as humans in subsequent eras, and their evolution has continued apace. As for the dinosaurs that became extinct, someday in your not-too-distant future they will reappear when your scientists learn how to clone them from fossilized DNA."

I was fascinated at this glimpse of an ancient human civilization that was so different from my own, and I wondered what our world would be like today if they had survived. Imagine a society where there was no technology. What would people do every night if they couldn't watch their favorite mind-numbing TV dramas or cloying sit-coms? And, Heaven forbid, what would our teenagers do if they couldn't text? They would have to look each other in the eye and converse verbally, just like their out-of-touch parents and grandparents. What a hellish world that would be, indeed.

Oh well, enough digressing for now, I thought, as I focused my attention back to Albert.

"Watching this civilization function so peacefully and in harmony with nature, in sharp contrast to our modern-day civilization, raises another obvious question, Albert. Are there human civilizations on planets other than Earth?"

"I was wondering when you would get around to this question. There are indeed human civilizations on other planets, some of which are more advanced than your civilization and many that are more primitive. The planets they inhabit are similar to Earth since the human body can only exist within certain environmental parameters. It was all part of the Galactic Council's grand experiment to seed humans wherever they could thrive and monitor their development.

(The Galactic Council, as Albert had explained in *Dancing Forever with Spirit*, was the governing body of the federation of planets in our galaxy. One of their duties was to oversee the seeding of life on planets in the Milky Way when they were capable of harboring life.)

"Come with me and I will show you a couple of examples that exist right now in your current time."

We left the Hall of Records and exited Aglaia through its main entrance portal, passing through the lush meadow on our way out of the Spirit Side. Albert clutched my arm and pointed toward a cluster of stars close to Ursa Major. The stars blacked out momentarily before reappearing again, except now the Earth and the Moon were no longer visible. Instead, we were floating high above a blue planet with two large land masses surrounded by oceans. The planet was orbiting a yellow star that looked much like our sun when seen from Earth, only larger.

I was keen to see another human civilization in action, and I hoped I would not be disappointed. Little did I know I was about to witness a shocking scene of misery and hopelessness.

Chapter Nine

Marching to a Different Drummer

We floated down through the cloudless sky of the blue planet and landed on a broad plain near the edge of a chain of mountains. The land was covered with lush vegetation that was not like anything on Earth. The foliage was mostly light blue, with clumps of yellow and orange flowers scattered over the landscape. Near the edge of the mountains I noticed a thick forest of tall trees and shrubs gently swaying in the breeze.

Albert guided me toward a cave opening in a nearby mountain that led to a large cavern carved out of the rock. It was illuminated with hundreds of burning torches hanging from sockets chipped into the stone walls. Off to the right was the opening of a smaller shaft that created a passageway into the mountain. We proceeded toward the bustle of activity near the center of the chamber, and my jaw dropped with surprise.

I saw a line of humans walking in single file, each carrying two large buckets laden with some type of ore. They were naked except for a skimpy loin cloth and shackles on their ankles. They were all men, with stringy black hair, scraggly beards, and layers of black dirt sticking to the rivulets of sweat running down their pallid torsos. They shuffled slowly toward a queue of large wooden carts where they would empty their buckets and head back to the mining shaft for another load.

At strategic spots along the human chain their slave masters watched them with disdain, cracking their long black whips on the bare backs of anyone who stumbled and fell. The slavers looked like something out of a science-fiction movie. From the neck down they looked like humans, with light brown skin and black body hair, except they had cat-like heads with short furry ears and yellow fangs. Their feline faces were twisted with hate-filled grimaces as they seemed to enjoy lashing red welts on the backs of the men who felt their fury.

We left the cave and headed down the hill toward a cluster of small hovels built from mud. The village was surrounded by a ten-foot-high wooden fence with sentry towers along the perimeter. Inside the compound women were tending to the cooking fires and preparing food. They wore drab and threadbare sarongs that seemed to complement their despondent countenances. Their infants were lying nearby in tattered blankets, and the older children huddled sullenly beside the fires. Their evening meal was always a thin gruel made from the handful of vegetables they were allotted each day.

At sundown the men from the chain gang were escorted into the compound and released from their shackles. They trudged slowly to their huts where they were greeted warmly by their families. After wolfing down a small bowl of gruel, they would crash on one of the straw mats in the shacks, exhausted from the hard labor in the mine.

"What is this place, Albert? Who are these brutes, and why have they enslaved the humans?"

"This is Cronus, a planet many light years from Earth. These humans were seeded here long ago by the ETs under the direction of the Galactic Council. They lived happily in their primitive civilization for eons until the slave drivers arrived from another continent. The slavers were aggressive and brutish by nature, and they lived with constant violence in their society. They first traveled to this land a few decades ago in their sailing ships and discovered a mineral they needed to make weapons. Because they were more advanced than the indigent humans, with superior weapons, they were able to enslave the humans to work their mines.

"As you can see, the humans here have a miserable existence with no joy or hope in their lives. The men work in the mines day after day without any time off, and the women are confined in this compound to cook, clean, and raise the children. Luckily for them, their life expectancy is very short."

"Why don't the ETs do something to stop this abuse?"

"Because this was a life experiment designed by the Galactic Council to observe the development of two different, but similar, life forms that were seeded simultaneously on two different continents on this planet. The dominant race was created by genetic mutations that resulted from the combination of human and feline DNA. The terms of this experiment dictated that no one was to interfere with the developments on this planet, even if the results turned out to be abysmal for one of the life forms. As you can see, the slavers developed much more quickly than the humans, but without any parallel advances in emotional intelligence. It is a sad situation, and there is a petition right now before the Council to allow the ETs to transport the humans to another planet in order to put an end to this travesty, although we may not know the outcome for some time."

It was very distressing to observe the plight of these humans, but there was nothing I could do to help them. So I signaled to Albert that I wanted to leave, and followed him back into an orbit around the planet. Albert pointed his arm toward another star cluster, and we sped off as before, with the stars disappearing for a few seconds before coming back into focus.

We were now hovering above a green planet that looked like Earth, except the land masses were different. Albert led me down through the clouds until we landed in a meadow lush with green vegetation and dotted with colorful, fragrant flowers. I did not recognize any of the plants, but I very much enjoyed the splendor of this stunning vista with its many different hues of green glistening in the bright sunlight. We headed toward a city in the distance, with its gold and silver tower spires reaching toward the clouds. It looked like one of the futuristic cities I remembered from one of the *Star Wars* episodes.

When we reached the main entrance to the city, I paused for a few moments to take it all in. The streets were filled with tall humans with dark-brown hair, green eyes, and bronze complexions. The men wore identical black jumpsuits made from a soft and supple fabric, with shiny black boots covering their feet and ankles. The women all wore silver jumpsuits made from a metallic fabric, along with soft white boots that rose up past their calves.

The humans were riding on the moving people conveyers that lined the edges of the street, one going in each direction. Overhead I could see dozens of flying vehicles of various sizes that sped between the gleaming towers. It seemed chaotic, but I surmised they all must be controlled by computers to avoid collisions.

Albert and I hopped on the conveyer that was headed toward the center of the city. When we entered a large public square we disembarked and strolled toward the large imposing edifice at the far edge of the square. It was a magnificent building with white marble pillars and wide stone steps leading to the main entrance. We made our way through the arched doorway guarded by shiny brass double doors and ambled down a long hallway that ended at the edge of a large circular chamber lined with rings of seats. Sunlight streamed in from the large skylights that circled the huge domed ceiling.

Albert explained that we were on the planet Thraso. The building we were in was the seat of the government for this civilization, and he brought me here to meet the reigning Empress, Marpesia. Even though this planet was on the same dense-matter dimension as Earth and our astral bodies could not normally be seen by the citizens, Albert had arranged for us to meet with the astral body of Marpesia so she could see and hear us.

The chamber was empty except for a regal woman seated on a gold throne in the middle of the chamber. She motioned for us to approach and be seated on two royal-blue velvet-covered chairs lined up in front of her throne.

"Greetings, Marpesia. As agreed, I brought a human from the planet Earth to meet with you," Albert began.

"Peace be with you, Albert and Garnet," Marpesia responded with a smile. "How can I be of service today?"

"As you know, I asked Albert to bring me here so I could learn about human civilizations on other planets," I replied. "I am very curious about your civilization. Can you tell me how your society functions?"

"It would be my pleasure," Marpesia responded. "Let me start by describing how we operate today, and then I will give you a brief history of how we got here."

"We are a matriarchal society governed by women. Women hold all the political offices in our society as well as all of the decision-making and managerial positions in education, commerce, and science. Men are subservient to women in every sense, but we are not cruel to them. We do not subjugate men—we just don't allow them to assume any position of importance. They are free to work, if they choose, or to spend all their time in artistic and recreational activities. They can roam our streets and the countryside with impunity and live free and happy lives. They are treated with kindness and compassion and do not lack any of our material comforts.

"Our society is democratic and egalitarian for all women. The members of our governing Council are elected every four years by the women of our society. Men are not allowed to vote. The position of Empress is selected by a vote of the members of the Council every four years, and an incumbent Empress cannot serve more than one term.

"We have a nonviolent society with no crime, conflicts, or wars. Every citizen has free access to everything they need for nourishment, shelter, and entertainment, so there is no jealousy over status or material possessions. We are able to immunize ourselves from all known diseases, and medical science has become very adept at healing injuries caused by accidental traumas. And because we have learned how to slow down the natural aging process, the life expectancy for our people is around 140 years.

"We live in peace and harmony with our planet and all of its creatures. We do not pollute our environment, and we do not eat animal flesh. We ingest food pills that are manufactured from vegetation that grows abundantly in our forests, which satisfy our hunger pangs and provide all the nourishment we need for a healthy diet.

"The key to the success of our society is our program to reduce testosterone levels in the men. We sterilize our boy children when they are three years old using a painless chemical treatment. We exclude some of the boys from this procedure to allow us to harvest their sperm, which is preserved in sperm banks. The reduced testosterone levels in our males make them docile and nonaggressive. As a result, they never harm other humans and are not prone to engage in fighting or other acts of aggression.

"The harvested sperm from our males is used to artificially incubate eggs in one of our birthing centers. The babies are lovingly cared for by our nursing staff and then educated by the women instructors in our schools, but they never know the identity of their biological parents. Girls are educated separately from the boys to ensure they are taught the leadership skills they will need when they become adults. Women and men do not form relationships or engage in sex. Our men are totally uninterested in sex, while our women, if they are so inclined, can enjoy sexual activities with other women.

"Our society was not always like this. Several thousand years ago we were a patriarchal society ruled by aggressive and violent men who cruelly subjugated women and treated them like chattels. Women were not allowed to work or to vote, and they were expected to cook, clean, raise the children, and be sexually pleasing to their men. They were not allowed out of their homes except when accompanied by their husbands or another male relative. And if they were disobedient in any way, their husbands could beat them with impunity.

"In those days, our society was rife with crime and violence, and wars were a common occurrence. It was truly a nasty society, especially for the women.

"Then we enjoyed a critical shift in the structure of our society. One of our women, Andromache, who is idolized now by our citizens, had a vision one night while sleeping. She was told the polemusa plant that grows in our forests would drastically reduce the testosterone level of any man who ingested its leaves. And the woman in her vision encouraged Andromache to gather these leaves and spread the word to all other women. This movement started slowly but gradually gained traction. Surreptitiously over a period of several years the women fed the polemusa leaves to their men. The results were astonishing, as women gradually converted their society from one ruled by violent men to one governed by kind and compassionate women. Our society today is the end result of that breakthrough many years ago."

"This is quite a story, Marpesia," I responded. "How do you avoid disagreements or conflicts among the women in your society?"

"We do have some disagreements, but they are always settled amicably without any lingering animosity. We know we are all eternal souls connected to the Source, and we have conquered the illusion of separation. And because everyone in our society has free access to all the material goods they could possibly need or want, there are few reasons to quarrel."

"What about the men in your society?" I wondered. "You say you are not cruel to your men, yet you take away their manhood at an early age, and you don't allow them to assume any position of importance. Isn't this subjugation?"

"Spoken like a man from a patriarchal society. In truth, our men do not miss their sex drive because they never remembered having it. They are raised in a society where women make all the decisions and assume all the responsibility, and they think this is the natural order of things. They cannot imagine things being different, so they have no desire to alter the structure of our civilization. They enjoy carefree lives free from strife and conflict, with nothing to worry about. They can go to school, work at low-level jobs, pursue artistic endeavors, and participate in many different sporting and recreational activities. Wouldn't you prefer this lifestyle to the one you have on Earth?"

"That is certainly one way to run a planet, although I think there must be a happy medium between the patriarchal extremes of my planet and the radical matriarchal policies of your world. I thank you for sharing your story with me, and I wish you and your fellow citizens all the best in your future endeavors."

I felt an urgent need to leave this planet before Marpesia decided I should experience the joys of being a eunuch in her world. I sincerely hoped this civilization would not learn how to travel between the stars before I had a chance to warn the men back home, lest we all end up singing like the Vienna Boys' Choir.

Albert and I waved good-bye to Marpesia and left the chamber. My head was spinning with a host of conflicting thoughts. I had a lot of information to digest, and I realized my quest to see other human civilizations was far more distressing than I had bargained for. It was enthralling, however, to observe these very different human civilizations scattered throughout the galaxy, and I hoped one day Albert could show me more of these intriguing human societies. In light of what I had seen, I wondered where my civilization would end up if it managed to survive. Time would tell, no doubt.

Albert seemed to sense my bewilderment, so he guided me back to my home on Earth. But before he left me, I had a question for him.

"You mentioned before, Albert, that souls who incarnate on Earth aren't restricted to lives on this planet, and they can incarnate into physical life forms anywhere on the dense planes. Did I have any previous lives on the planets we just visited, or on any other planets?"

"You did not have any lives on these two planets, although you did incarnate into many different life forms on other planets before you began your journey on Earth. Most of them were relatively uneventful compared to a human life on Earth, but there is one particular incarnation you may want to explore in the Akashic Records. It is a good example of a life-seeding experiment by the Galactic Council that went awry. It will demonstrate clearly that life in the universe will often develop in unpredictable ways despite the careful planning of the flora and fauna architects."

Albert quickly disappeared through the ceiling, leaving me puzzled by his last remark. I had a sense of foreboding about my next trip with Albert, hoping I had not been part of some ill-considered experiment that had ended tragically.

Chapter Ten

Paradise Lost

When Albert fetched me two days later we paused briefly at our usual rendezvous point high above Earth. I loved soaking up the scenery from that vantage point and felt grateful to be able to enjoy the serene beauty of all the stars in our galaxy. What a monumental task it must have been for the Source to create a universe so large and diverse and with so many different life forms populating the billions of planets in all the galaxies. It was almost beyond comprehension—something my puny human brain might never fully understand. I was thankful I would return to the Spirit Side when I passed from this life because there I would regain the knowledge and wisdom I previously enjoyed as a being of energy, an individual aspect of the Source. And then, maybe, I would be able to fully appreciate the magnificence of the Source.

My musing was interrupted when Albert tugged at my sleeve, signaling it was time to continue our journey. We trekked back to the Spirit Side and into the Hall of Records where we found an empty viewing room and sat down beside the globe with the blue and white swirls. Albert waved his hand over the sphere and a new vista filled the globe.

I was peering down at an azure planet that looked much like Earth, with continents interspersed with oceans and lakes. As the scene zoomed down to the surface, its multicolored vegetation came into focus. Some of it resembled the trees, shrubs, and grasses that were common on Earth, but most of the plants were unfamiliar. There were trees with yellow bark and purple leaves, tall grasses with triangular leaves that rippled with red, white, and blue stripes, and shrubs displaying saucer-shaped black blooms covered with silver polka dots.

The scene in the globe panned over the landscape, and I noticed a group of animals nibbling on the grass. They reminded me of the wild mustangs that still roam the foothills and plains of North America.

Albert pointed to a newborn colt that was standing on wobbly legs for the first time.

"You incarnated into this little colt a long time ago after discovering this planet on one of your astral expeditions. What you are seeing is the result of a unique experiment organized by the Galactic Council. This planet originally housed only plants that had been imported from other planets, including Earth. As the next step in its evolution, the Council seeded it with a variety of life forms from elsewhere in the galaxy, including several species, like the mustangs you see here, from Earth. The original mandate from the Council dictated that only herbivores could be seeded here; no carnivores or omnivores were allowed. This arrangement worked out very well at first as all the creatures prospered and multiplied without any fear of being eaten by other animals.

"You had an idyllic, but uneventful, life on this planet that seemed at first blush to be a herbivore paradise. After the initial success of this experiment, however, things began to fall off the rails."

Albert waved his hand over the globe and the scene morphed to a view of the planet many years later. The animals I had noticed from the earlier scene were still there, except the landscape looked much different. The bodies of all the animals that had died from old age were scattered everywhere, their flesh still intact. In some places the carcasses were so thick that walking among them was difficult.

Albert said the mandate from the Council that no flesh-eating life forms could be seeded on this planet had worked all too well. It meant there were no microorganisms that consumed dead animal flesh anywhere on the planet. The microorganisms that decomposed vegetation were present to ensure that dead plants were recycled back into the soil, but this was not the case with the flesh and bones of dead animals. Hence the animal carcasses continued to pile up and blot the landscape.

When the Council saw the outcome of their experiment they realized corrective action had to be taken before the dead bodies snuffed out all life on the planet. So they seeded this world with microorganisms that thrived on dead animal flesh to take care of all the bodies. This solved one problem, but it kick-started another complication for the peaceful, plant-eating creatures who roamed the planet.

Albert moved the scene in the sphere forward in time to a date several eons later. The vegetation looked the same, but the grazing animals that had once dominated the planet were few and far between. The globe zoomed in on a small herd of mustangs galloping across the plain in a frenzy. They were running from a pack of black animals that looked like large weasels. They were as large as Labrador retrievers and as swift as greyhounds. They soon caught up to the trailing mustang that staggered and then fell from the weight of the hunters on its back. The pack devoured the mustang with great relish before moving on to find their next kill.

"The carnivores in this scene are the direct descendants of the flesh-eating microorganisms introduced to take care of the carcasses," Albert explained. "Life in the universe often has a funny way of charting its own course that cannot always be anticipated. Over time, the flesh-eating microbes mutated and evolved into the weasel-like predators you just saw in action. This was not expected by the Council, but they are bound to follow their own directive to let life on this planet play out without any interference."

So much for the thought that a world without carnivores would be paradise, I mused. Although my life on this planet was short and uneventful, now I understood my affinity for horses on Earth. And from now on I wouldn't be nearly as offended if someone said I was the north end of a horse going south.

The vista in the globe gave way to the customary blue and white swirls. It was fascinating the way the Source, as the master architect of the universe, continued to surprise and confound the life forms it created with eventualities that were beyond the ken of even the most intelligent of its creatures. The universe never ceased to amaze.

I looked at Albert, hoping he could help me make sense of what I had witnessed on my recent expeditions.

"It seems, Albert, that the Galactic Council has been very busy with its life-seeding experiments throughout the galaxy, and many of them do not work out exactly as planned. From what I understand, they seeded Earth with humans, on several occasions, and much of the sea life found in our oceans and lakes. And they enlisted the help of several races of ETs to plant the seeds and monitor the progress of the life forms on our planet.

"And you had mentioned before the ETs have also provided assistance and inspiration to humans from time to time throughout our history, some of which has been the stuff of legends. I am curious about human contact with the ETs, and I wonder if you could show me a few episodes in this saga."

Albert furrowed his brow, and then responded: "There have been thousands of ET/human contacts over the ages, and someday you will be able to return here to view as many of them as you like. For now, we must continue to follow the agenda I have set out for you, even though you would rather do other things. But I will let you sneak a peek at a couple of encounters that will explain a few of the unsolved mysteries that have intrigued humans for quite some time.

"The first one you will see happened a long time ago on the Salisbury Plain in England, at the place you now know as Stonehenge."

Chapter Eleven

Visitors from the Stars

Albert waved his hand over the holographic globe and the blue and white swirls morphed into a new panorama. It was a flat plain covered with short grass and clover, with a few clumps of beech trees scattered here and there.

Albert indicated we were looking at the Salisbury Plain in England, circa 3000 BC. He said he would show me scenes from one of my previous lives as a Druid priest, whose name was Fagus.

As the scene in the globe zoomed in, I could see a solitary figure facing the morning sun. He was wearing a coarse hooded robe cinched at the waist with a rawhide cord. His jet-black hair and neatly trimmed beard framed a rugged face with piercing amber eyes peering out from a brooding brow.

And then my perspective shifted, and I was living as Fagus once again. I remembered now why I was standing all alone on this plain. The night before I had a very vivid dream where Andraste, the goddess of victory, appeared before me to deliver an important message. She told me I had to journey to this spot the next morning to meet a special emissary from the stars, and I should follow his bidding. So I had hastened to this location as soon as I rose in the morning, eager to meet this celestial envoy.

I watched the sun rise slowly in the east until I heard a whirring sound to the west. I turned to see a large silver globe slowly descend from the sky until it was hovering only three feet above the plain. After several minutes the whirring stopped, a rectangular door slid open on the underside of the sphere, and a short staircase unfolded to the ground.

Although I was fascinated by this silver ball, I was apprehensive about what would happen next. I didn't have to wait long before a humanoid being appeared at the door and descended down the ladder. He looked like a human except he was taller than any man I had ever seen, likely eight feet from his head to his toes. His golden hair lay plastered to his large head in tight curls and his hazel eyes sparkled in the morning light. He wore a billowing white blouse and a burgundy skirt that resembled a kilt. The bulging muscles on his arms and legs rippled as he strode in my direction. I stood there frozen in my tracks, unable to move as I admired this magnificent specimen. This was, no doubt, the envoy I was supposed to meet.

My apprehension faded as soon as he flashed a warm smile, his perfect teeth gleaming in the sunlight.

"Greetings, Fagus. I am pleased you got the message from Andraste. I am Mogons from a star system in the Andromeda constellation. My race is closely related to the humans on Earth. We originated from the same seed stock eons ago, although our physical attributes are larger in scale than humans on this planet because of the peculiar nature of the radiation emitted by our sun. Our larger brains allowed us to advance our technology more rapidly than your race, and our spaceships can easily travel throughout our galaxy.

"I am here to enlist your services as our point man for a cosmic beacon to be built on this site. We are not permitted to build it ourselves because the galactic directive mandates these sites be built by the indigenous people who live nearby. But we can provide guidance and assistance to make the job easier."

"What is a cosmic beacon?" Fagus asked.

"A cosmic beacon is a navigational aid for interstellar travel. It provides a directional guidepost for spacecraft when they are in warp drive and conventional guidance systems are inoperative. Your planet, and this site in particular, are on one of our galactic ley lines that make it a strategic signpost for travel to this part of the galaxy. It is necessary to build this beacon so my race and other galactic races can more easily navigate between the stars in this sector."

"I don't understand everything you have told me, although I am willing to do my part to help," Fagus offered with some hesitation. Fagus didn't know what he was supposed to do, but he expected he would soon find out.

Mogons unfurled a roll of parchment and spread it out on the top of a nearby boulder. It was a diagram showing several concentric circles of massive standing stones joined by horizontal lintels. Inside the stone circles was a group of thrilithons composed of two vertical stones topped with a lintel. The diagram contained details about the types of stones to be used in this structure and the location of the northeastern entrance, which precisely matched the direction of the midsummer sunrise and midwinter sunset for that location. The back of the parchment depicted what it would look like when finished. From my perspective in the viewing room, I recognized it immediately—it was Stonehenge.

As I once again watched the scene play out before me, Albert waved his hand over the globe to speed up the action. Fagus had gone back to his village with Mogons to recruit the villagers for the building project. Fagus explained to them that Mogons was a god who had come down from the stars to help them build a sacred site for worship. They were in awe of Mogons and quickly agreed to do his bidding.

Mogons was very particular about the stones he wanted for his project: bluestones from the Preseli Mountains and sarsens from Carmarthenshire, both in Wales. Although neither of these locations was close at hand, Mogons insisted on using these stones because they had special subatomic properties that were necessary for the proper functioning of the beacon.

Because these stones, which weighed several tons each, had to be transported a long distance from the quarry, this building project would never have been completed without some technological help from Mogons. He provided Fagus with two magical tools to aid the process: one was a laser cutting tool that could be used to carve the stone blocks from the wall of the quarry, and the other was a wand that could nullify gravity around any object.

With these tools, Fagus and his countrymen were able to easily carve out the standing stones and lintels and move them to the Stonehenge site where they were placed with precision in accordance with the detailed instructions from Mogons.

As the scene continued to unfold in fast time, the cosmic beacon was soon completed, looking exactly like the structure in Mogons's diagram. The final step was the positioning of the power source for the beacon, a small metal box Mogons had fetched from his spaceship, in the center of the structure.

Mogons left once the cosmic beacon was finished, leaving the Druids to use the site for religious ceremonies and burials. Little did they know the stone circles played an important role in the navigation of our galaxy.

When the scene in the globe reverted to blue and white swirls, Albert explained that Stonehenge had functioned as a cosmic beacon for several centuries even though the local people used it as a ceremonial site. When the power source for the beacon was depleted, Mogons returned to the site to retrieve it. It was not necessary for him to install a new power source in the structure because he had built another beacon on one of the moons of Jupiter, making Stonehenge redundant in the scheme of things.

Because Mogons left with the diagram and the tools used in the construction of Stonehenge, modern archeologists have not been able to discover the true origin and purpose of the stone circles. Someday, according to Albert, Mogons's race from Andromeda will return to Earth to welcome humans into the galactic federation. But this will happen only when our race has renounced its violent ways.

"What an enthralling look at the origins of Stonehenge, something archeologists have been trying to determine for years," I said at last. "There have been some people who have speculated that ETs were involved in the construction of Stonehenge, and now I know for certain. And now I am anxious to see the other ET encounter you promised to show me."

Albert nodded his assent and waved his hand over the globe once more. The blue and white swirls in the globe dissipated, revealing a bucolic landscape sweltering in the hot afternoon sun. It was a semiarid plain with patches of buffalo grass, prickly pear cactus, and other scrubland flora. Far off on the horizon I could see the heat waves rising slowly.

Albert said this was the high plains of New Mexico, about seventy-five miles from Roswell. It was early July of 1947, and Albert revealed I was about to witness firsthand a much-talked-about historical event.

I watched the unchanging scene in the globe for several minutes, not sure what to expect. Then out of the blue a saucer-like object plummeted from the sky and smashed into the side of a small arroyo. It kicked up a cloud of dust as it bounced up and skidded to a halt a hundred yards past the initial impact zone. (Thanks to Albert's deft hand at the controls of the globe, I was able to watch this action in slow motion.)

The scene in the globe zoomed in to provide a close-up view of the saucer. It was a metallic disc about fifty feet in diameter and twenty feet thick in the center. The outer edge of the disk was punctuated with a row of round portholes, but I could not see any other markings on its smooth surface. Albert focused the globe on the inside of the craft, which looked much like the cockpit of the space shuttle. There were three padded chairs aligned in a row in front of the instrument panel. And strapped into the chairs were three small humanoid beings.

The little crew members were about three feet tall, with arms, hands, and legs similar to humans. Their hairless heads were slightly oblong in shape, with the lower portion descending to a rounded chin. They had large oblong eyes, delicate little noses, and thin pursed lips. They wore jumpsuits made of a shiny metallic material and black boots that looked like synthetic rubber.

Albert told me I had just witnessed the crash of a spacecraft piloted by ETs from the planet Gorgon, which was located in the Pieces constellation. They were part of an observation vanguard that had been monitoring Earth ever since the first fission bomb had been exploded, which had attracted the attention of this alien civilization. Their mission was to observe the activities of humans and report their findings to their superiors on their home planet. This spacecraft was a scouting vehicle based on a large mother ship orbiting the Earth.

As I looked more closely at the occupants of this craft, I noticed two of them were motionless, while the one in the center was moving its arms and emitting soft moaning sounds. The animated alien touched several buttons in the control panel, and I heard a loud swoosh of air as a doorway opened on the lower surface of the craft. The survivor tried to rise up from its chair but the effort was too much, and it sank back down into the padded seat, unable to negotiate an exit through the open door.

Albert waved his hand at the globe to compress time, and I noticed a small convoy of two army jeeps and a truck come to a halt beside the saucer. The officer in charge advanced cautiously toward the craft and entered through the open doorway. He quickly assessed the situation and ordered the troops to carry the aliens on stretchers to the back of the truck. Once loaded, the truck sped off toward the Roswell Army Air Field, while the remaining soldiers guarded the crash site. Later that afternoon the saucer was loaded onto a flatbed semitrailer truck with the help of two large portable cranes. It was covered by a canvas tarp and hauled away to an empty hangar at the Air Field.

Then Albert shifted the scene to a secluded and heavily guarded hangar at the Air Field. I could see a team of doctors working on the sole survivor, who now lay motionless on a hospital gurney. After several hours of intense procedures, the doctors realized they had lost the battle, and they covered the little body with a white sheet.

Albert waved his hand once more over the globe, and it returned to a swirl of blue and white vapors.

I had plenty of questions for Albert. "I assume what I just saw was the famous UFO crash in Roswell in 1947? What happened to the little aliens and their spacecraft?"

"This was indeed the famous Roswell crash. The little scout craft had been on a reconnaissance mission to observe a high-altitude surveillance balloon launched by the U.S. military as part of a top-secret program named Mogul. As it approached the balloon at a high speed, its advanced propulsion system inexplicably failed, causing it to crash into the balloon payload. The collision knocked out an essential component of the craft's guidance system, which caused the spacecraft to crash into the desert below.

"The military denied the existence of a flying saucer (despite several eyewitness accounts to the contrary), and when they displayed the crash debris to the press it was indeed the wreckage from the balloon, as they claimed. What they didn't disclose, however, was the existence of the saucer that had crashed a few miles from the site of the balloon wreckage. The spacecraft was transported under heavy security to Roswell Army Air Field, then to Edwards Air Force Base, and finally to the secretive military base known as Area 51 in Nevada, where it remains hidden to this very day. The saucer was constructed of a super-strength metallic alloy that allowed it to survive the crash without major structural damage. Your scientists have extensively analyzed the alloy, but they have not yet been able to decipher its composition. Likewise, they have not been able to understand the nature of its propulsion or avionic systems. In short, the military engineers have still not been able to figure out how this spacecraft functioned.

"As for the crew of the scout craft, two of them died on impact from injuries to their internal organs. The third one survived for several days, eventually succumbing to its injuries despite the valiant attempts of the medical team at the Air Field. Their internal organs were not too dissimilar to those of humans, but the damage had been too extensive and they had not been able to save the little guy.

"All three corpses were flown to Edwards Air Force Base where autopsies were performed. Later the bodies, still immersed in preservative chemicals, were transported to Area 51 where they remain today.

"The existence of the spacecraft and its crew has been denied by the U.S. government ever since the 1947 crash. The cover-up was authorized initially by high-ranking military officers, and all subsequent U.S. government administrations have sanctioned the blackout on the basis the public did not need to know the truth."

"What about the mother ship?" I asked Albert. "What did they do about the crash?"

"The mother ship was aware of the crash, but they were not able to mount a salvage operation for the scout ship or its crew. They were under strict orders from their home planet to ensure they were not observed by humans, so a rescue/salvage operation was out of the question in light of the tight military security around the wreck. They were relieved when they realized their spacecraft would not be put on public display."

"Did the survivor say anything before it died?"

"It did try to speak to the humans who pulled it from the spacecraft, but its verbal language was unintelligible to the soldiers. The little alien did draw a small sketch on a notepad before it died—a dove holding an olive branch in its beak—an ancient symbol for peace."

"What a captivating story, Albert. Am I free to disclose the truth about Roswell?"

"Go ahead, but don't expect everyone to believe your story. Someday the truth will be revealed to the public by the U.S. government, although that time has not yet come. In the meantime, I thought you might like to meet one of your pioneer space travelers who had an ET encounter of his own."

The chance to meet a space pioneer really piqued my interest. As a child I had been captivated by the early American space program, often feigning illness so I could stay at home to watch the launches and capsule recoveries on television. I was so keen that I wrote a speech about Alan Shepard, the first American in space, when I was in the fourth grade. I recited my speech in my school's oratorical contest and managed to come in first. (Fortunately for me I was the only one in the contest.)

We left the viewing room and Albert led me out of the Hall of Records and back onto the main boulevard of Aglaia, which was busy as usual. We strolled at a casual pace until we came to a small park nestled among the shimmering white buildings. Sitting beside the water fountain in the center of the park was a solitary figure I did not recognize at first. When we got closer my heart skipped a beat as I realized I was going to meet one of my childhood heroes: Neil Armstrong, the first man on the Moon.

Chapter Twelve
Man on the Moon

Neil Alden Armstrong looked the same as when he had returned from his Apollo 11 flight in 1969. He gave me his famous boyish grin as I shook his hand. I was thrilled to meet him, and I could hardly wait to hear his story.

"It is a pleasure to meet you, Neil," I began. "And I am dying to find out about your brush with the ETs."

Neil sat down next to me and began his tale: "It is nice to meet you as well, Garnet. Albert filled me in on your current mission on Earth, and I volunteered to meet with you to disclose some details about our Apollo 11 mission that I could not reveal on Earth.

"Our mission to the Moon has been documented extensively ever since we arrived back on Earth. What you have read or watched in the news media is basically correct, but the real story lies with the extraterrestrial encounter I had on this mission that has never been reported. It was an event I kept to myself for all those years after I returned to Earth, even though the truth was bursting to get out.

"It happened just after the Eagle had touched down on the Sea of Tranquility. While Buzz and I were going through our landing checklist and getting ready for our walk on the Moon, I heard this voice in my head:

Welcome to the Moon, Neil Armstrong. Do not be alarmed—you are not losing your mind or hallucinating. My name is Lassa, and I am speaking to you telepathically. You are the only person who can hear me, and I recommend you do not let anyone else know about our conversation lest they think you have become mentally unstable.

I am a being from the planet Selene which orbits a star many light years from Earth. We have developed advanced technology that allows our spacecraft to fly faster than light. We have been observing your civilization on Earth ever since the Wright brothers took their first flight, and we are especially interested in the progress your civilization has made with your recent spaceflights. We expect someday humans will travel to other planets in your solar system and eventually to other stars.

I am speaking to you from our underground base on the Moon, which has a well-concealed entrance portal on the far side of the Moon. Our mandate is to observe your activities without being detected by humans; hence we are very discrete when we monitor your space excursions. My contact with you is an exception to this rule because landing a man on the Moon is a very momentous event for your race. My race still commemorates that day thousands of years ago when our space pioneers first traveled to our closest moon.

We want to extend our congratulations, Neil, on this historic achievement. This will be our only direct contact with humans, but we will continue to covertly monitor the progress of your space program. We look forward to the day when humans will develop a warp drive that will allow them to visit the stars, and maybe even visit my home planet.

When you first step off the ladder to walk on the Moon, look down and to your left about ten feet from your craft. We left a message for you—a little sign to let you know we are for real and you are not hallucinating. Farewell, Neil, and enjoy your adventure.

"And that was all. I tried to speak to her telepathically because I had umpteen questions, but I got no response. So I returned to the task at hand without saying a word about this to Buzz or Mission Control.

"When I finally stepped down on the surface, I walked a few steps to my left. Sure enough, just as Lassa had said, I noticed a message etched in the fine dust that blanketed the surface: *Welcome to the Moon, Neil Armstrong.* I quickly erased the message with my boot and turned around to watch Buzz climbing down the ladder.

I never disclosed my contact with Lassa or the message in the dust to anyone because I did not want this historic event to be tainted with allegations I had mental health issues. I took this secret to my grave, but now I want the truth to be revealed."

"This is a spellbinding story, Neil," I responded. "It must have been difficult for you keep it under wraps for all those years. Did you ever have any doubts about Lassa and the things she disclosed?"

"There were times when I wondered if I had only dreamed about my contact with Lassa, but the memory of this event was so vivid that

I knew it had been real. And after I passed over to the Spirit Side I reviewed this time period in the Akashic Records. Sure enough, my encounter with Lassa did happen, exactly as I described it to you. I have watched this episode many times, and I am still thrilled about my adventure on the Moon so long ago. And I also saw her underground base on the Moon, which is still operating. I marvel at their sophisticated technology and hope humans will someday be able to travel to the stars, just like Lassa."

I lingered for a while longer, enchanted by Neil's saga about his life of fame as the first man on the Moon. Then we bade Neil farewell, and retraced our steps back to the main street and the bustle of the crowd.

Albert revealed the details about our next rendezvous as we walked: "We have a date to meet with two giant historical figures who enjoy a special niche in the chronicles of human civilization on Earth. One of them has been adored as a god, while the other has been vilified as an evil monster. I hope you are ready for this, because you will be very surprised to see them sitting side by side."

Chapter Thirteen
Strange Bedfellows

I eagerly followed Albert through the maze of streets to the edge of Aglaia where we came upon a pastoral meadow with a burbling stream snaking its way through the lush green vegetation. In the distance I noticed two individuals sitting on a bench by the brook, seemingly engaged in an animated conversation. As we got closer my jaw dropped open as I recognized the characters on the bench: one looked like Jesus Christ and the other closely resembled Adolf Hitler.

Albert and I sat down on a nearby bench and waited for them to notice us. After several minutes the soul who looked like Jesus turned to face us with a warm smile.

"Greetings to you both. And thank you, Albert, for arranging this meeting. Just as you surmised, Garnet, I am the soul who incarnated on Earth as Jesus Christ. This good soul beside me last incarnated as Adolf Hitler. We meet here regularly to discuss our past lives on Earth and the impact, both good and bad, we had on your planet during our lives and in subsequent times.

"You look surprised to see us sitting here side by side because you only remember our historical lives on Earth. To you we are like polar opposites, and you find it difficult to comprehend how the two of us could be engaged in an amicable conversation. This is precisely why Albert brought you here today. We want you to better understand the cycle of life on Earth and the interaction of souls on the Earth plane and on the Spirit Side.

"We know you will have questions for us, so we are here at your disposal."

I sat there quietly, still overwhelmed by these two larger-than-life historical figures. *Where to begin?* I wondered. After an embarrassing silence as I struggled to regain my wits, I managed to stammer out my first question: "How is it possible the two of you—one the embodiment of love and peace and the other the personification of evil—can sit here side by side and have a pleasant conversation? You can't mix oil with water."

"We get that a lot," Jesus responded, "especially from newly arrived souls who have not yet regained their full awareness of the reality of life in the Spirit Side. From your conversations and astral trips with Albert, you should realize by now what happens on Earth stays on Earth, except for the wisdom gained from a life on your planet. As you know, the Source does not make rules for humans to follow on Earth, and nothing that happens on your planet is right or wrong in an absolute sense. So while you may view me as a good guy, and Adolf as a bad guy, the reality is that we are both souls created by the Source who incarnated on Earth to grow and evolve or to help others with their journeys. What we did while on Earth does not affect our status as individual aspects of the Source, which loves everything it has created unconditionally."

"What you tell me, Jesus, tracks what Albert has been trying to knock into my thick skull ever since I first met him. Intellectually I accept this concept, but emotionally it is more difficult to swallow. It is my problem, however, and I will have to deal with it in my own good time. In the meantime, I have many questions for both of you. Where should I start?"

"You can start with me," Adolf chimed in, "and if it is all right with you, I would like to change out of this ridiculous uniform, which I wore only so you could recognize me easily. And please call me Mathew— the name I use on the Spirit Side." As he spoke, Mathew morphed from a mustachioed Hitler in military uniform to a handsome young man in a white robe.

"Tell me about your life on Earth," I continued. "Did you plan all of your atrocious activities before you incarnated?"

"For the most part, no. I did plan the significant aspects of my life, like my place of birth, the people who would be my parents and siblings, and the other people who would have the most influence on my life. When I chose my parents I also knew the most likely outcome for the physical, intellectual, and emotional characteristics of the human baby I was about to enter because of the predictability of human genetics. How I turned out was not guaranteed, although I assumed my human form would follow the genetic trend.

"Within the framework of those initial parameters, my Life Plan called for me to become involved in politics, using my leadership and oratorical skills to propel me into a position of authority, even if I did not know precisely where that would lead me. I had hoped my political aspirations would allow me to help my people recover from the ravages of World War I, but I knew all bets were off once I incarnated as a human.

"As Albert has told you, when souls incarnate into human bodies they are like resident observers. They experience everything that happens to the human body, except they do not control the actions of their human. They must try to influence the human mind as best they can with subtle messages, most often through intuitive flashes, nighttime dreams, and gut feelings. But human minds do not always hear or recognize the messages for what they are, or they find a way to rationalize a different course of action.

"Since humans are not allowed to remember where they came from or what they intended in their Life Plans, and because they are given the free will to make decisions and take actions, they will frequently stray off course, sometimes with drastic consequences. These are huge challenges for souls incarnating on Earth and the reason your planet is one of the toughest schools in the universe.

"Free will is the major wild card in the lives of all humans. Their free will actions are often dictated by emotions as they react to the events they encounter in their day-to-day lives. And whenever humans let their negative emotions, like fear, anger, and hate, get out of control it often results in violence and bloodshed. And when souls are planning their lives on Earth they cannot predict with any accuracy how their human minds will ultimately use this freedom of action.

"To get back to my life as Adolf Hitler, I did not plan his evil deeds before I incarnated. What transpired in that life was a classic case of a human mind totally ignoring the messages it got from its soul and its spirit guides and letting emotions rule the day. In the case of Hitler, fear and hate dominated all other emotions, which led to the horrible atrocities committed by the Third Reich. As the soul occupying that body I was frustrated at my inability to influence my human mind, although there was little I could do other than brace myself for a stormy ride.

"You should understand, however, that Hitler was not alone in his evil endeavors. He was encouraged and supported by powerful men with a similar mindset, like Himmler, Goering, Goebbels, and Hess. As you know, human emotions can feed on other emotions, often coalescing into a mob mentality with disastrous consequences.

"After my death on Earth, I had to spend time in a reentry hospital to deal with my evil life and my overwhelming guilt. After my initial recovery I spent a long time in my Life Review going over every aspect of my tragic life. And then I was allowed to meet the souls of some of my victims, who gave me their unconditional love and forgiveness. When I was finally able to forgive myself, I was ready to move on and continue with my evolution."

I sat there mesmerized by his tale, not sure how I should respond. I needed time to digest what he had said, so I decided to move on and direct my next question to Jesus: "Now it's your turn, Jesus. Why did you incarnate on Earth?"

"The Council of Wise Ones had decided humans were in need of a kick in the pants to get them back on the right track," Jesus began, "and they asked me if I would incarnate on Earth to help the cause. I was happy to do so, and the rest is history."

"Did you plan to be crucified? Did you know you would be the genesis of a new religion that would play a major role in world affairs after your death?"

"I intended to preach love and compassion to the masses, with the hope that those who heard me would be converted to my cause. I was endowed with the ability to utilize the energy of the universe to perform miracles so I could attract the attention of my disciples and the citizens of my country. We expected I would be successful in winning people to my cause, and this would ruffle the feathers of the religious elite. So while we didn't know exactly how I would meet my demise, we thought it likely I would be persecuted for challenging the authority of the holy men of my country. My crucifixion was the end result, and it succeeded in making me a martyr for my beliefs.

"We hoped my teachings would continue in some form after my death, and the beginning of a new religion was the desired result. We could not predict how it would all unfold after my death, but the end result was Christianity, which developed over the centuries following my death."

"Since you had the ability to perform miracles, why did you not use your powers to escape your crucifixion?" I queried.

"I could have escaped from death on the cross, but it was not something I wanted to do. In that incarnation I was allowed to remember who I was, where I came from, and my plans for that life. I knew I would be going Home after my physical death, so I was not afraid to die. I also knew my demise would have the most impact if I died in a dramatic fashion, and my crucifixion and subsequent ascension fit the bill nicely. My martyrdom was an inspiration to my followers in the years after my death."

"When you left this incarnation, did you anticipate Christianity would follow the path it has taken so far?" I asked.

"The exact path for the Christian Church was not foreseeable back then, given that its evolution has been dictated by humans who have free will to follow their own earthly agendas. And the agendas of the men who developed the rules and dogmas of the Church did not always coincide with the truths I left for humanity when I walked the Earth as a human. This was no surprise to me or the Council of Wise Ones—since we knew all too well humans often succumbed to the weakness of the flesh as they struggled to make sense of their journeys on your planet.

"Much to my chagrin, the leaders of the Church made a lot of missteps along the way, which frequently resulted in the senseless torture and killing of innocent people whose only crime was worshiping a different God. If they had only focused on what I had preached to my followers this violence could have been avoided. But that is water under the bridge, and it cannot be changed.

"On the plus side, Christianity has had a huge impact on human civilization since my time on Earth, and most of it has been positive. It provided a spiritual nudge up the evolutionary ladder that was needed at the time, and it has given comfort and hope to billions of people all over the world."

"Many Christians eagerly wait for the second coming of Christ. Will you return to my planet to save us from the wicked people who live among us?" I wondered out loud.

"I have no present plans to do so, but I am at the beck and call of the Wise Ones. Only next time, if there is one, I don't want to be born in a manger. I think a suite in a five-star hotel would be more suitable. And forget about the frankincense and myrrh, I would rather have champagne and caviar."

"I beg your pardon," I sputtered.

"Just joking," Jesus said with a wink and mischievous smile, as Albert and Mathew guffawed with great delight. I had to keep reminding myself that humor was alive and well on the Spirit Side. When the merriment died down, Jesus and Mathew bade me farewell and disappeared behind a thicket of trees. I was disappointed to see them leave, and I hoped I could meet with them again someday to finish the conversation.

I turned to face Albert, wondering what he planned for me next. I soon found out he had another surprise up his sleeve when he spoke at last.

"Since you seem to be keenly interested in the biblical tales of holy men who performed miracles to inspire their followers, I thought you might enjoy meeting one of the towering figures from the Hebrew Bible, the man who parted the Red Sea so his people could escape from the Egyptian army."

Chapter Fourteen
It's a Miracle

Before long I noticed an old man with a long white beard shuffling toward our bench. He had piercing blue eyes that intimated great wisdom. Albert hugged the old man and invited him to be seated.

"Greetings, Moses," Albert began. "Thank you for joining us today. I wanted you to meet my friend Garnet, who is still living on Earth. I asked you to join us today because he wants to know more about the miracles described in the Bible."

Moses shook my hand and smiled at me with a twinkle in his eyes.

"Are you really the Moses from the Bible? The man who parted the Red Sea to save his people?" I cut to the chase.

"I was Moses during my last life on Earth," our guest responded.

"I am puzzled—you don't look much like Charlton Heston."

"I know, I get that a lot. I may not be as good looking as Chuck, but I think I have an aura of righteousness that makes up for it."

"Did you really do all the things they attributed to you in the Bible, or are they just allegories created by the scribes?"

"In truth, it is a bit of both," Moses conceded. "My mission in that incarnation was to lead the Israelites out of slavery, provide them with a new set of laws, and persuade them to adopt a new monotheistic religion, now known as Judaism. Because I had enjoyed many previous lives on Earth the Council of Wise Ones recruited me for this role. I did not have to accept this assignment, but I did so willingly in an effort to help the people I had lived among in several earlier lifetimes. I felt a moral obligation to steer the Children of Israel on a new path of salvation.

"Some of what is said about me in the Hebrew Bible actually happened more or less as described, while other parts were fabricated or embellished to make a better story. When the Bible says God spoke to me on Mount Sinai, it was actually my spirit guides who were reminding me about my mission on Earth—which was to go to Egypt to free the Israelites from slavery and lead them to the Promised Land. The burning bush that was not consumed by fire was staged to get my attention, something to shock me into action.

"The biblical description of the ten plagues visited on the Egyptians was mostly correct except for the last one—the slaying of the Egyptian firstborn males. No innocent babies were actually killed, but we terrified the Egyptians with the delusion of that slaughter. I convinced the Egyptians the plagues were caused by our God, who was a supreme being with great powers. In fact, I conjured up the plagues by tapping into the energy of the universe with the able assistance of the good spirits back Home, much like Jesus did when he performed his miracles. This little ploy worked, and the Pharaoh let my people leave before he changed his mind and pursued us with his army."

"And did you actually part the Red Sea so your people could pass through?" I wondered.

"I actually created an interdimensional passageway that allowed my people to trek from one side of the Red Sea to the other without getting wet. And contrary to the biblical accounts, the Egyptian army did not follow us into the Red Sea and perish when the walls of water collapsed. That part was added by the scribes who felt this would finish the story with a sense of justice.

"As for the Ten Commandments, these laws came to me after several days of deep meditation as I channeled messages from my guides. I convinced my followers they came from God because I knew this would have more force and affect than if I told them I authored the laws after deep meditation. This was my way of inserting some moral fiber into this group and sowing the seeds of a new monotheistic religion."

"You have a fascinating story, Moses. Do you have any plans to reincarnate on Earth?"

"Not at this time, but I am willing to go if called upon. The people of Israel and Palestine seem to be mired in conflict, and it may take a special effort from someone here to bring peace to that region. I will have a chat with Mohamed to see what we can come up with."

Moses rose to leave and waved good-bye, while Albert led me back to the main boulevard of the city. As we strolled down the street

I heard cheering and applause coming from the direction of the amphitheater where I had enjoyed the John Lennon and George Harrison concert on a previous visit. Impulsively I headed toward the clamor, eager to see what the fuss was all about, while Albert trailed behind me with a look of resignation on his face.

When we reached the amphitheater I noticed the seats were filled with people in their colorful garments. On the stage below was a full orchestra forming a semicircle around a conductor who was gracefully waving his baton to direct the music. Albert said the man with the baton was the soul of the man who wrote the music during his last incarnation on Earth. It was none other than Wolfgang Amadeus Mozart, one of the most prolific and acclaimed composers of the Classical era. The orchestra was staffed by former members of the Mannheim Orchestra who had played many of Mozart's compositions during their lives on Earth.

The music was alluring and uplifting, unlike anything I had heard on Earth. I was in awe of this master composer, and thrilled to see him in action so long after he had passed from his last life in Austria. The adoring audience was captivated by the sheer artistry of this performance, with many standing and shouting "bravo" at the end of each piece. It was a perfect combination of masterful music compositions and impeccable execution—enhanced by the grandeur of everything on the Spirit Side. And in response to a chant from the crowd, Mozart finished the set with his magnum opus: Symphony No. 40 in G minor. The standing ovation seemed to go on forever, much to the delight of a beaming Mozart.

I wanted to stay in the amphitheater for the next concert, but Albert indicated the fun had come to an end—at least for the time being. Reluctantly I followed Albert out of the stadium and back onto the main boulevard.

As we strolled down the street, my thoughts turned back to the meetings I had with Jesus and Moses. I understood now how they had performed their miracles, and I wondered if it was still possible for humans today to tap into the energy of the universe to perform miracles like these Masters did while on Earth. I raised the question with Albert, and he had a ready response.

"Jesus and Moses did not have a monopoly on creating miracles, although they are certainly two of the best-known practitioners of the art. There have been many miracles performed over the years, both before and after the glory days of those great men, by people who had also learned to utilize the power of focused thoughts. In a lot of cases their feats went unreported because these sages preferred to live in relative obscurity.

"Come with me back to Earth and I will introduce you to a modern-day guru who has learned to levitate through meditation and focused thought. It will be good for you to see that biblical miracles are still in vogue, even in the twenty-first century."

We left the Spirit Side and zoomed down toward Earth, landing in northern India. We touched down near a small Buddhist monastery and proceeded through the main gate.

"This is a Buddhist monastery that was established here in the 1960s after the Dalai Lama fled Tibet," Albert explained. "One of the monks living here has mastered the practice of focused meditation. He has been a monk since his childhood years and has spent much of his life in a deep meditative trance. I wanted to show you how meditation can enhance your spiritual experience on Earth by focusing your thoughts on what is truly important on your journey."

Albert led me down the main hallway to a small room at the back of the monastery. An old monk was sitting on a thin cushion in the center of the room, his legs crossed in a lotus position with his hands resting palm-up on his thighs. His eyes were closed and his breathing was shallow, like he was in a trance.

According to Albert, through meditative concentration this monk had learned to levitate, pass through walls, and communicate by telepathy, which are two of the six types of higher knowledge sought by all Buddhists on the path to attaining nirvana.

"Through deep meditation this monk has learned to use much more of his brain than the typical human, and this allows him to tap into the vast energy of the universe. It is the same technique Jesus Christ used to perform his miracles, and it has been utilized over the centuries by many other people who have gone mostly unnoticed. Because they didn't intend to gather followers to start a new religion, like Jesus, the other humans who mastered this art chose to remain obscure, since they had no desire to attain fame or fortune."

I watched the old monk in silence, not knowing what to expect. After several minutes, my eyes opened wider in wonderment as he began to rise off the mat until he was floating a foot off the floor, with no visible means of support. Then his frail body began to rotate counterclockwise, spinning slowly for several minutes before halting back at his starting position facing us. Suddenly his eyes popped open, and he gave me a wink and a smile. It was obvious he could see and hear us, even though we were in astral form.

"Welcome, Albert and Garnet," he said telepathically. "Are you surprised to see me levitate?"

"I am," I responded. "This is not something I get to see every day. How do you do it?"

"By focusing my thoughts and concentrating. Thoughts are like beams of energy that can manipulate energy and mass. Focused thoughts are much more powerful, just as a laser beam is more powerful than the beam of light from a flashlight. Most humans have thousands of thoughts every day, which are scattered helter-skelter in all directions. This is why most humans cannot levitate, walk through walls, or communicate by telepathy. Focused thoughts, on the other hand, can affect mass on the denser planes in ways that seem miraculous to those who have not mastered this technique.

"Occasionally, ordinary humans can achieve such results on a temporary basis when an urgent need arises. You have probably heard stories about people suddenly acquiring superhuman strength that allows them to lift a heavy beam that has fallen on their child, only to realize later they could not even budge the same beam under normal conditions. In these situations, the emergency they confronted caused them to de-clutter their minds and focus on one powerful thought, which was to lift the beam and free the child.

"After many years of practice I have learned to focus my thoughts through meditation, and this allows me to manipulate mass on this plane in ways that seem magical. My path is not an easy road to follow, which is why most humans will never master these skills."

"Why don't you demonstrate your powers to the whole world?" I wondered. "Our scientists would love to see you replicate these feats in their labs."

"I won't because I don't wish to become a circus freak. And I do not need or want any publicity or public adoration. I am quite content to remain here in obscurity to continue my quest to attain nirvana."

With a nod of his head the little monk closed his eyes to continue his meditation. Albert and I floated up through the ceiling and back to our rendezvous post high above Earth.

"This was an example of someone using meditation to create miracles," Albert continued. "But these results are extremely difficult to achieve. For most humans, they should be happy if they can use meditation to eliminate worry and stress, discard their negative emotions, and become better at listening to their spirit guides. And the miracles can wait because everyone can easily perform these feats once they are back on the Spirit Side."

What Albert said made a lot of sense. It was fascinating to see what the old monk could do by focusing his thoughts, although I understood his path was not for everyone. So I resolved to continue to practice meditation when I got back home in an effort to sweep away my worries and fears and focus on the positive things in life. Too bad I couldn't buy a mind purgative at the drugstore—it would be so much easier.

Albert escorted me back home to my mundane life so I could chronicle my recent adventures. He told me he would return in a couple of days to resume my journey of enlightenment, because, as he liked to remind me, I still had a long way to go. He was concerned I was still too judgmental about other people, and I needed to enhance my capacity to empathize with those souls who had lived evil or depraved lives on Earth. To that end, he announced he had arranged for me to meet a few souls who had experienced sinful or nefarious lives in recent times, including one who had been a violent terrorist.

I was not sure what to make of this, so I braced myself for his next visit, hoping I would be able to conceal my disdain for the lowlifes I would soon meet.

Chapter Fifteen
Violence and Revenge

When Albert returned three days later we scooted back to Aglaia and strolled down the busy boulevard, snaking our way through the teeming crowds.

I was always happy to visit the Spirit Side with Albert, not just to take in the wonderful ambiance of Aglaia and the surrounding countryside, but to meet all the interesting souls who had completed their lives on Earth and were back Home enjoying the break between incarnations. Albert had introduced me to many souls who had interesting stories to tell, and each one had a unique message for me to pass on to all humans. Albert didn't randomly select souls for me to meet—he carefully planned these events to give me an opportunity to gain new insights about the cycle of life on Earth and the evolution of souls in this tough school.

We ambled down one of the side streets of the white city until we arrived at an unadorned, two-story building with brick steps leading up to a large wooden door. We entered through the main entrance, crossed the foyer, and made our way down a long hallway punctuated with doors on either side.

"This is one of the reentry hospitals in Aglaia," Albert explained. "It is a convalescent home for distressed souls who have recently returned from the Earth plane. It is for those souls who need extra care and attention because they had a traumatic death on Earth or lived their last days with a lot of pain or mental anguish. They are provided with counseling and guidance from volunteer souls who had been in the healthcare or counseling professions on Earth and from souls who had been patients here themselves in the past. The patients are wrapped in a cocoon of love and compassion that helps them deal with the memories of the trauma and pain they suffered in their last lives. And in cases where a soul had been the perpetrator of heinous crimes, they are taught to release their residual guilt and forgive themselves for their misdeeds.

"No one is forced to come here, but they are encouraged to do so if they are having difficulty making the transition from the Earth plane. No souls are ever forgotten or abandoned, and all souls who check in to this hospital will eventually return to the mainstream on the Spirit Side.

"I brought you here to meet one of the patients. His name is Ahmed and he recently arrived here after a tumultuous life in the Middle East. He belonged to a terrorist group and was instrumental in killing hundreds of innocent men, women, and children during his short and stormy incarnation. He was killed in the Israeli/Hamas conflict in Gaza in 2014, and when he returned Home he was in a state of confusion, bewildered by his new surroundings and laden with self-condemnation for the atrocities he had committed. His guides brought him here as soon as he crossed over, and he has made remarkable progress since then."

Albert stopped in front of one of the doors and knocked softly before we entered. It was a small room with a single bed against one wall and two hard-backed chairs along the opposite wall. Seated on the bed was Ahmed, wearing a white terry-cloth robe and soft cotton slippers. Albert and I sat down on the chairs as we silently contemplated the man on the bed.

Finally Albert broke the silence: "Greetings, Ahmed. This is my companion, Garnet, who is here in astral form. He is still living his life on Earth, and I brought him here so he could hear about your troubled life on Earth and learn to accept other souls for what they are, without judgment."

"Greetings to you both," Ahmed responded cheerfully, "and welcome to my humble abode. What would you like to know?"

I took this to be my cue, so I began: "Can you give me a brief history of your life on Earth?"

"Of course," Ahmed replied, as he began his spellbinding tale of violence, hatred, and revenge.

"I was born in the mid-eighties to a Palestinian family living in the Gaza Strip. I was the youngest of four children, with two brothers and one sister. My father was a merchant who owned a pottery store, and my mother worked long hours cooking, cleaning, and raising her children. We were devout Sunni Muslims who prayed often at the local mosque. We did not have a lot of money, but we lived a happy life full of love for each other and devotion to Allah.

"And then one evening when I was seven my comfortable world suddenly unraveled. I had been playing with a friend a few blocks from my home when I heard a loud explosion nearby. I raced home to find my house in shambles and completely engulfed in flames. I stood there shaking with terror as I could not see anyone from my family on the street. One of my neighbors noticed me and wrapped her arms around me in a tender hug. She was sobbing as she told me our house had suddenly exploded, and she feared everyone else in my family had perished. The kind lady took me to her house and offered me food, but I was not hungry. I spent that night on a small cot where I eventually cried myself to sleep.

"The next day I learned everyone in my family had been at home when disaster struck, and none had survived. The news reports said our house had been hit by an errant rocket launched by the Israelis toward a terrorist hangout a few blocks from our house. Israel asserted the attack was retribution for the rockets the terrorists had lofted into Israeli settlements the day before.

"I went to live with my mother's sister and her husband, who also lived in Gaza. They were kind people who treated me well, but I never forgot the horror of watching my family and my home go up in flames. My rage grew by the day, and I yearned for the opportunity to exact revenge for the massacre of my family.

"When I was twelve I ran away and joined the Izz al-Din al-Qassam Brigade, which was the paramilitary arm of HAMAS, eager for a chance to avenge my family. I lived in one of their command posts in Gaza and quickly learned how to shoot an AK-47, launch a grenade, and make a pipe bomb. Our targets were the Israelis, who had killed so many of our people over the years, and the Americans, who were their biggest supporters.

"My first kill came when I was fourteen when a pipe bomb I had planted by the side of a road exploded, killing two Israeli civilians. I grinned wickedly as I watched the two men burn inside their vehicle, but that did not slake my thirst for revenge. Instead, I felt exhilarated at my success and eager to kill again. And so I did—several more times in the next couple of years. Never once did I feel any shame or remorse. I was on my own personal crusade to inflict as much damage as possible on the enemy.

"When I was fifteen I traveled to Afghanistan with a friend to enlist in a terrorist training camp. This was the big leagues compared to the group in Gaza. The training camp schooled its recruits in all the latest terrorist techniques— recruiting and equipping suicide bombers, building sophisticated explosive devices, and planting bombs on airplanes and subway cars. I spent hours and hours learning how to kill in hand-to-hand combat and many more hours studying the most effective ways to massacre large groups of people. After six months of rigorous training I was ready to return to Palestine to continue the war.

"Back in Gaza, my terrorist cell was very active and I was happy to be part of it. I became very adept at recruiting naive citizens, often teenagers, to strap bombs to their bodies, slip into a market or restaurant in one of the Israeli settlements, and blow up dozens of innocent people. It was surprisingly easy to find recruits, and the bombs were a very effective way of killing the enemy and striking terror into the hearts of their citizens.

"The end for me came when I was only twenty-eight. I was killed during the Hamas/Israeli conflict in the summer of 2014 when an Israeli missile struck our rooftop laden with rocket launchers. As soon as I left my shrapnel-riddled body my guides cradled me in their arms and brought me to this hospital, where I have been cocooned by the attentive staff. As you can imagine, I was very messed up on Earth, and I needed a lot of tender loving care when I crossed over from the physical plane."

Ahmed paused for a few moments to catch his breath, while I tried to soak up what I had just heard. I had more questions for Ahmed, so I began my interrogation: "Why did you feel the need to kill all those people, Ahmed?"

Ahmed was pensive as he tried to collect his thoughts. "Initially, my need to kill was fueled by my insatiable desire to avenge my family's death. I hated the Israelis for launching their missile, and it didn't matter that my house was not the intended target. They had killed my family and turned my world upside down, and I vowed to make them pay.

"After my thirst for revenge had been mostly satiated, I was driven to kill in a quest to manipulate and control other people. I took delight in causing havoc because it gave me a feeling of great power when I could cause huge disruptions in the lives of many people with a few well-placed bombs. It was a power trip like no other, and I was addicted to the thrill of the kill.

"I was not a religious fanatic like many members of my group. Most of my fellow terrorists actually believed the religious propaganda we were fed on a daily basis. Our leaders constantly reminded us that Allah wanted us to kill the enemy, and we would be rewarded handsomely in Heaven if we did his bidding. To them, blowing up innocent women and children was not wrong in any sense because Allah had commanded them to do so.

"I never bought into any of that nonsense. In fact, I didn't believe in Allah or in any other supreme being. I had no personal use for religion, but I did recognize its usefulness in controlling other people. I had learned how easy it was to manipulate feeble-minded people into doing your bidding as long as you convinced them it was Allah's will they do so. Even something so inherently abhorrent to most people, like killing young children, could be justified if Allah desired the end result.

"What amazed me the most was how so many people could be so gullible. They believed the propaganda their religious leaders fed them without asking any questions or having any second thoughts. They swallowed this hogwash hook, line, and sinker, without any qualms— confident Allah would provide them with an eternity of bliss in return for their service.

"The leaders of the terror and rebel groups were very well versed in this paradigm, and they used religion very effectively to achieve their goals. But you need to understand it is not just modern terrorists who use religion to con others to carry out their agenda of violence, because this manipulation of the masses has been going on for much of human history. Christian holy men used this tool with great success centuries ago when they recruited loyal Christians to join the crusades to the Holy Land, where they were incited to burn villages and kill innocent women and children in order to carry out God's desire to drive the infidels from the birthplace of Christ. And thousands of innocent Jews were tortured and killed during the Spanish Inquisition by Christians who believed they were following God's commands.

"So the control and subjugation of people through religion has been going on for a long time. Christians should not take a holier-than-thou view of what today's religious extremists are doing—because they are using the same tools deployed so successfully by Christian holy men centuries ago."

When Ahmed paused to gather his thoughts, I jumped in with my next question: "Why was it so easy to recruit people to commit horrible acts of violence? Whatever happened to their innate sense of right and wrong?"

"Not everyone we approached came over to our side," Ahmed admitted, "but we always managed to find enough people to do our bidding. They were the ones who were able to suspend their moral code of conduct because they believed they had the ultimate form of justification for their crimes—Allah's blessing for their actions. And they were often encouraged by their families who were convinced these suicide missions would please Allah and make them heroes of the Palestinian people."

"So what do you think about your life now that you are back on the Spirit Side?" I wondered.

"I have not yet had my full Life Review, but after many discussions with my counselors I now have a much better understanding of the life I just completed. I know I put myself into that life to learn how to control my hate and anger, although I failed this test miserably. I totally ignored the messages from my guides and took delight in my ability to block out any feelings of remorse or shame for my evil deeds. Subconsciously, I knew I was wrong and I wished my life would end so I could quit the killing. I had a death wish that spurred me to take on ever-more risky missions until the Israeli's finally granted my wish with their missile attack.

"I understood when I was devising my Life Plan that the tests I had planned would be difficult to pass, but I was brashly confident I could overcome all the obstacles. Now I see the light, and I realize I bit off more than I could chew. I am keen for another chance on Earth to see if I can do better, except next time I will map out a life with less turbulence and more love, and maybe then I will have better control of my negative emotions."

"I came here today, Ahmed, thinking I would not enjoy meeting you because of your wicked past. Now I can see you are a soul, just like me, who got off on the wrong foot in his last life and was never able to recover. After hearing your story, I am confident you will be able to exorcize the demons from your last life and continue to grow and evolve as a soul."

Albert signaled it was time to leave, so I hugged Ahmed good-bye and left the hospital. Ahmed's tale was a chilling example of how things can quickly get out of control in a vicious cycle of violence and revenge. Everyone on Earth needed to hear his story so they could avoid the same pitfalls and understand that the bad guys are just souls having a human journey that veered off course and degenerated into a life of depravity. As Albert liked to remind me, all souls return to the Spirit Side no matter what they did while on Earth. Everyone gets a free pass to Heaven.

"Ahmed's story was an eye-opener for me, Albert. What surprised me the most was he knew deep down inside that what he was doing was wrong, but he couldn't bring himself to stop. Instead, he developed a death wish—hoping someone else would put him out of his misery. In the end, the Israeli missile granted his wish in a fiery explosion. Was Ahmed effectively committing suicide by his reckless actions?"

"People can commit suicide in many different ways," Albert responded. "In most cases they take deliberate action to end their lives by ingesting poison, jumping off a bridge, or blowing their brains out with a handgun. Sometimes the action is much more subtle, like refusing medical treatment or putting oneself into a dangerous situation with little hope of survival. Ahmed knew full well that continuing his terrorist ways would likely end tragically, but he thought it would be more virtuous to die at the hands of the enemy than to put a bullet in his head."

"I can understand why Ahmed chose to end his life the way he did, Albert, because no one is ever praised for committing suicide (except if you are a suicide bomber). All the religions condemn it as a sin, and most people regard it as a contemptible act of a cowardly person too weak to face the harsh realities of life. I am troubled by the whole concept, and I would like to explore the true nature of suicide. Do you think we can take a time out from your rigid agenda?"

"No problem, because I expected we would get to it sooner or later. Go ahead and ask away."

Albert was being so agreeable that I wondered what devious scheme he had up his sleeve this time. Past experience told me I would soon find out.

Chapter Sixteen

A Life Cut Short

As we strolled down the streets of Aglaia, I decided to take advantage of Albert's offer to answer my questions about suicide.

"You told me before in one of our earlier dialogues, which I described in *Dancing on a Stamp*, that suicide was not wrong in any absolute sense because there were no absolute right or wrong actions on the Earth plane. Since the Source does not make rules for us to follow, nothing we do on Earth, including suicide, will make us unworthy to fulfill our roles as individual aspects of the Source. Even though suicide is not wrong in the eyes of the Source, it often results in a life being terminated far too soon, with many learning opportunities wasted.

"You also told me our souls have the right to determine when our physical bodies die, and no one dies by accident. But I am having trouble reconciling this concept with death by way of suicide. When people commit suicide have they usurped their soul's right to determine the date of their death?"

Albert, as usual, was ready with his answer. "A soul always has the right to pick the date its physical body dies, even when suicide is the cause of death. Sometimes suicide is an exit point planned well in advance by the soul. There are several reasons a soul might choose suicide to exit from an incarnation, although most often it is intended to provide tough life lessons for the family of the suicide victim. In these cases the suicide was included in the Life Plans of all the souls who would be affected by it, including the family members left behind.

"In other situations, however, suicide is not a planned event and the soul must struggle with its human mind to stop this act of self-destruction. This usually happens when people become so distraught with the circumstances of their lives that they cannot be dissuaded from using suicide as an escape from their pain, and their souls realize a continuation of those lives would be fruitless. At this point, souls will throw in the towel and agree to allow the suicide to proceed. It is very frustrating for souls when this happens because all the remaining learning experiences they had hoped to encounter in those lives have fallen off the table. It is a wasted opportunity they will have to include in another incarnation.

"This is not an easy concept to grasp, and it will help if you can speak to someone who committed suicide in one of their past lives on Earth."

We made our way to the main plaza in the center of the city and parked ourselves at one of the tables. The large square was filled with laughter and animated conversations from the diverse collection of spirits dressed in colorful garments. I loved the energy of this place and was quite content to idle away my time free from all concerns about timetables and deadlines.

My reverie was soon interrupted when a handsome gentleman dressed in a navy-blue business suit, white shirt, and red paisley tie approached our table. Judging by the gray hair on his temples I guessed he was in his early fifties.

"Garnet, I would like to introduce you to Edward, who committed suicide in his last life on Earth. I think you will find his story interesting," Albert announced, as I reached out to shake Edward's hand. After taking a seat at our table, Edward began his story.

"As Albert pointed out, I did commit suicide in my last life. It was a tragic finish to what had otherwise been a happy and fulfilling life. It all came to an end when I started my car in my garage with all the doors closed. Death came quickly, and I crossed over to the Spirit Side immediately, eager to leave that life behind. After spending some time cocooning in the reentry hospital, I completed my transition and went through my Life Review, which was troublesome to watch in several places.

"Before I go any further, I think it will be useful for you to understand the circumstances that led to my self-inflicted demise.

"I was born into a middle-class family in Melbourne, Australia. My parents were good people who loved their children dearly and who always encouraged us to do our best in all of our endeavors. I graduated from high school at the top of my class and went on to university, finishing with an honors degree in geology. I married my high-school sweetheart, Alice, and began my career with a large multinational mining company. I quickly rose up through the ranks and was the senior manager in charge of one of the mining divisions at the time of my death.

"Alice and I had three bright and talented children, Emily, Ethan, and Charlotte, and life was very good to us. We had a nice house in an upscale suburb of Melbourne and we took many delightful family vacations in Europe and North America. We were a close family that enjoyed spending time together at home and abroad.

"I was very ambitious and driven to succeed, and I always wanted to be in control of the events in my life. My wife used to tease me for being a control freak, but that term actually suited me very well. And patience was never one of my strong suits, even from my early days as a child. In my view, things never happened as quickly as I thought they should, which resulted in a lot of frustration in my otherwise happy life.

"And then when I was fifty-one, with two of my kids in college and the youngest one in high school, my world came crashing down around me. After noticing blood in my stool one morning I sought a diagnosis from our family physician. Numerous tests later, my worst fears were confirmed: I had advanced colon cancer that had metastasized to other organs in my body. They gave me six to eight months to live.

"After my initial shock I became very angry. 'Why is this happening to me?' I shouted at God. In my opinion I had done nothing to deserve this treatment and it was grossly unfair. But God did not reply, and I was left with the bitter realization that my time was running out. My family was very supportive, and they encouraged me to fight the cancer and not give up hope. My doctors wanted to slow the growth of the cancer with chemotherapy and radiation, although I couldn't see the point in prolonging things. If I was going to die in six months what was the use in trying to hang on for two more months?

"One of the most troubling aspects about the whole situation was that I had no control over the end result, which was infuriating to someone like me. I was going to die when the cancer chose to snuff out my life, and there was nothing I could do to stop my inexorable march toward death.

"Then one morning a solution popped into my addled brain: I could control the timing of my death if I took my own life before the cancer could summon the grim reaper. The more I thought about it, the more I liked the idea of cheating cancer out of another victim. So one afternoon when the kids were at school and my wife was out doing errands I took matters into my own hands. The last thing I remembered before the carbon monoxide filled my lungs was the faces of my wife and children—and I realized then I was making a big mistake.

"Until I had my Life Review I didn't appreciate how devastating my death was to my family and friends. I hadn't intended to hurt them, but I could see and feel their heart-wrenching anguish in my review, and I understood how wrong I had been. I knew then my suicide was a selfish act designed only to satisfy my distorted need for control, without any regard for the feelings of the people I loved.

"To make matters worse, my guides told me during my review that if I had hunkered down to fight the cancer I would have enjoyed a miraculous remission, and my cancer would have been gone forever. If not for my precipitous action, I could have lived to the ripe old age of ninety-two. And when I saw the details of the Life Plan I had designed before I was born, I realized, much to my chagrin, I had missed some important life lessons because of my hasty departure. These missed opportunities would now have to be rescheduled for another life.

"My suicide also impacted the people around me in many ways. Not only did my family have to endure months of heartbreaking grief and shame, but they missed out on several life lessons their souls had hoped to encounter as they helped me win my battle with cancer and go on to become a proud grandfather.

"Needless to say, I wish I could go back and do things differently. That is not possible, of course, and I will just have to wait until my wife and children return Home to tell them I am very sorry for my selfish behavior.

"I hope you will tell my story to those still living on Earth, and maybe others in similar circumstances can avoid making the same stupid mistake."

"Thank you, Edward, for sharing your story with me. I will include your tale of woe in my next book, with the hope it may save someone out there from a similar fate."

I understood now why Albert had set up this meeting. He knew I was also somewhat of a control freak who did not count patience as one of his virtues. There was a take-away from this meeting aimed squarely at me, and I understood now that one of the lessons I had to learn was to accept that most things in life are not in my control because I am just one small cog in the giant wheel of the universe. And being impatient if events do not unfold as quickly as I would like demonstrates that I spend too much time anticipating the future instead of living in the present.

I decided I would start to change my thinking as soon as I got back home. For starters, I would stop watching the weather forecasts on television. I would not miss very much, since often the only accurate predictions they can make is a read-out of the current temperature. And who cares if I am out and about on a hot sunny day carrying an umbrella and a goose-down parka? At least I will be living in the present moment.

Albert seemed to read my thoughts about what I had learned from meeting with Edward. He gave me a knowing smile and a pat on my back as I waited for his next move. Albert was always one step ahead of me in more ways than I could imagine.

There was no doubt Albert had been on a tear recently. He had picked up the pace for his nightly visits, and I had a hard time keeping up with the chronicles of my astral treks. I was beginning to wonder if Albert was anxious to finish his mission with me so he could embark on a new assignment. He had been silent when I had raised the matter with him during our last excursion, so I resolved to brace myself for any eventuality he might spring on me.

After several minutes of quiet contemplation, Albert broke the silence.

"I have arranged for you to meet two souls who have recently finished very difficult lives on Earth. I want you to understand that judging other people is wrong no matter how repugnant they appear to be at first blush. One was a gay man and the other was a prostitute, and I hope you will be able mask your disdain and listen to them politely."

Chapter Seventeen
Judge Not Others

Before I could respond to Albert, a skinny man, who looked to be in his mid-thirties, approached our table. He was dressed in blue jeans and a white T-shirt, his gaunt face was pallid and blotched, and his dark-brown hair was cropped close to his head. We shook hands as Albert made the introductions.

"Garnet, I would like you to meet Jeremy, who wants to tell you the story of his last life on Earth."

"Namaste, Garnet," Jeremy began. "Thank you for meeting with me today. I understand you are one of Albert's messengers on Earth, and I hoped you would be willing to tell my story to the people of your planet.

"I am appearing to you today as I looked when I died from AIDS several years ago. I was a gay man who lived at a time when most people thought homosexuality was a sinful aberration that offended God and all right-minded citizens.

"I was born in the sixties in the Deep South of America, the so-called Bible belt. My parents were devout Baptists who attended church regularly and aspired to follow the teachings of Jesus Christ. I was the middle child of three, with an older sister and a younger brother. My parents were kind and loving to their children, but very strict about ensuring we always lived in accordance with their Christian principles.

"I was a tall, gangly kid who was gifted intellectually but not very good at sports. Although I always led my class academically, I was usually the last one to be picked for the sports teams at school. From an early age I displayed many feminine mannerisms, and I often felt more comfortable playing with the girls than roughhousing with the boys. As a result, I was bullied constantly by the other boys who taunted me for being a sissy. I had only one friend through most of my school years—a chubby Hispanic boy who was teased for being stupid and fat.

"To make matters worse, I often had an eerie feeling I didn't belong in my body—that I was trapped in the frame of a little boy by some weird quirk of nature. These feelings escalated as I got older, and I often caught myself staring dreamily at the cute boys in my class. I felt this was wrong, but I couldn't help myself.

"By the time I was in my mid-teens I could no longer delude myself—I was a homosexual. I had to keep this bottled up inside because coming out of the closet at that time would have been a disaster. My parents would have been horrified, and the other kids would have beaten me mercilessly.

"So I kept my little secret hidden from public view, as painful as it was. When I graduated from high school I eagerly accepted a scholarship at the University of California, Berkeley, where I would be close to one of the epicenters for gay men in America. I soon found many other openly gay men on campus, and my life blossomed like never before. The professors and other students did not care a whit about whether I was gay or straight, and I felt very comfortable with my sexuality.

"But I had not yet told my family about my sexual orientation, which was a dark cloud hanging over my head. So when I finished my freshman year I went back home to visit my family—determined to come clean once and for all.

"My family was dumbfounded when I told them, and their faces twisted into a mask of horror. Their reaction would not have been worse if I had confessed to being a serial killer. To make a long story short, my parents refused to accept me for who I was, and they told me to leave their house and never return. In their eyes, I no longer existed.

"So I scurried back to California to lick my wounds. I was devastated by their reaction because I still loved them very much and desperately wanted to be part of their lives. To dull the memory of that awful day of rejection, I turned to drugs, alcohol, and sex. I went on a promiscuous binge with many different partners over the next several years, ingesting drugs or booze on a daily basis to help me forget about my pain.

"I never did finish college, and I ended up waiting tables at a gay hangout in San Francisco. Eventually I settled down with a permanent partner, Billy, and I found a new groove in life. I had to be careful when I ventured outside of the gay community, as there were still far too many rednecks who taunted and bullied gays because they thought all faggots were a blight on society.

"I soon learned to tolerate this abuse, and I managed to feel good again about being in my own skin until I became very sick and was diagnosed with AIDS. My health deteriorated rapidly and my outlook on life dimmed just as quickly. I phoned my parents for the first time in years to tell them I was dying, but they refused to have anything to do with me. I died alone in my bed with only Billy at my side, my heart aching for a chance to see my family one more time.

"I want everyone to know homosexuality is not an aberration of nature, and it is not contrary to the laws of God. As you know, the Source does not make rules for humans to follow on Earth, and nothing it creates is a mistake. The Source created homosexuals the same as straight people, and they all have their own rightful place on Earth.

"When I returned Home after that life, I could once again view the Life Plan I had prepared before I was born. I realized then I had planned my life as a gay man in order to encounter some lessons that had spilled over from an earlier life when I had pummeled another man to death because he was a faggot. I wanted to experience life as a gay man to learn what is was like to be on the receiving end of homophobic intolerance.

"People need to understand that gays and lesbians are not abominations deserving of hate and ridicule. They are human beings with feelings and emotions who want to love and be loved just like everyone else. It is time for all humans to set aside centuries of misinformation and intolerance about homosexuals and embrace them as equal members of society."

"Thank you for sharing your story, Jeremy. I will do my best to disseminate your message to everyone back on Earth."

Jeremy waved good-bye and left the plaza, while I sat there quietly, waiting for Albert's next guest to appear. Instead, Albert got up and led me out of the city and into the lush green meadow on the outskirts of Aglaia. We followed a small stream that meandered through the gently rolling hills to the edge of the forest and sat on a wooden bench underneath a weeping willow tree.

"The soul you will meet next was a prostitute in her last life on Earth. Her name is Martha, and she has a story you need to hear."

"I am not really anxious to hear any sordid tales from someone who obviously had no dignity or self-respect, Albert. I would rather write about noble principles and ideals, about people who have overcome adversity to conquer the darkness. No one wants to read about the seamy side of life on Earth."

"I expected your reaction," Albert said with resignation. "But I insist you hear her story without making any hasty judgments."

And soon a pretty lady in a long blue calico dress approached our bench. Her long brown hair was pinned in a bun at the back of her head, and her full pouting lips glistened from a generous layer of bright red lipstick. Her hazel eyes twinkled in the sunlight, projecting the indomitable spirit of this proud and dignified young woman.

"Hello, Martha. As planned, I brought Garnet here to listen to your story."

Reluctantly, I rose up to shake Martha's hand. Her piercing gaze told me she knew what I had been thinking.

"Nice to meet you, Garnet. I understand your initial reluctance to meet a former prostitute, and I hope you will change your opinion of me after you hear what I have to tell you.

"I was born in 1831 in Pennsylvania in one of the Amish communities that populated that state. My parents were stalwart Christians who rigidly adhered to all of the Amish rules and traditions. My early life was very uneventful until I met a handsome young man named Isaac at one of our church socials. He was from a nearby Amish community, and his parents were also fiercely devoted to their religion.

"Isaac and I soon fell head over heels in love, despite the opposition by our parents to our proposed marriage. But we were not to be denied, so we decided to elope and leave our communities. We were shunned by both sets of parents, and they refused all further contact with us. So we headed west to find a new life for ourselves, eventually landing in a small frontier town in Nevada. Even though we had almost no money when we arrived Isaac found work as a deputy sheriff, and we were able to rent a small flat above the general store.

"Life was hard, but we were happy to be with each other and eager to start a family. Our firstborn was a girl, followed two years later by a baby boy. Life seemed to be treating us well despite the lack of contact with our families. We mailed many letters back home, but our parents never replied, even after getting news about their grandchildren.

"And then one fateful day my life began to unravel. Isaac was shot and killed when he tried to stop a bank robbery in town. I managed to hold him in my arms as he took his last breath, and I could see in his eyes that his love for me was never stronger than at that very moment.

"Things went from bad to worse after that tragic day. We had no savings, and I was unable to find any steady work in the town. I couldn't afford to move elsewhere, so I tried my best to make ends meet by doing odd jobs here and there. Times were tough in our little town, and even menial jobs like washing clothes or cleaning house were hard to come by. And asking my family for help was out of the question.

"I had to struggle to feed my children, who were now seven and five, and I was constantly behind on paying the rent money. I was terrified my children would be taken from me if we were evicted from our apartment.

"And then one morning, after my landlord gave me a two-week deadline to catch up on the rent, I realized that sometimes desperate people have to do desperate things. So I approached the madam who ran the brothel above the saloon about joining her little band of courtesans. Fortunately, I was young and pretty, so I was given a chance to try my luck at the oldest profession. The madam was a kind elderly lady who understood my circumstances, so she let me put my children to sleep in one of the unused bedrooms above the saloon where I could keep an eye on them.

"Initially I hated myself for stooping so low, but soon I was able to numb my conscience and zone out of reality during my nightly engagements with the paying customers. And because the money was decent I felt I had no choice except to continue until I had saved enough to fund a fresh start somewhere else.

"After a couple of years I had managed to save very little, and I feared I would have to do this forever. And then an angel came to my rescue. Nathan was a widower in his early forties who had a ranch a few miles out of town. His wife and only child had died two years before from tuberculosis, and he had been a regular customer of mine for the past year. He was a kind and gentle man who lived a lonely existence on the ranch that had once been filled with singing and laughter.

"Nathan shocked me one night at the brothel when he got down on one knee and proposed. He told me he had fallen hopelessly in love with me and wanted to spend the rest of his life as my husband and companion. Before I could respond, he said he would sell his ranch and move us to California to take up a new life—a place where nobody would know about my past.

"That was my ticket out of this place, and it would have been foolish to turn him down. Although I did not love Nathan, I liked him very much, and I believed I could grow to love him over time. Nathan was true to his word, and we all moved to the Central Valley in California where we purchased a small apple orchard. Nathan was a wonderful husband and provider, and he accepted my children as his own.

"When they were in their late teens, I felt a desperate need to tell my children about my history at the brothel. They were both sanguine about my confession, revealing that they had known about my work at the brothel all along without letting on. It seems they were taunted mercilessly at school for being children of a whore, even before they knew what the term meant. They hugged me tenderly with tears running down their cheeks, reassuring me in no uncertain terms that they loved me dearly and were proud of my fierce determination to do whatever was necessary to keep our family together.

"Nathan and I grew old together gracefully, delighted to watch our children marry and have children of their own. On my deathbed I thanked God for all the good things I had enjoyed in my life, as I slowly slipped away into the next world.

"So there is my story. I am not ashamed of what I did in that life, and if I had it to do over again I wouldn't change a thing."

"I am the one who should be ashamed, Martha, for passing judgment on you before I heard your story. I apologize for making hasty assumptions about you. I should have known better, but I all too often fall victim to the judgmental tendencies that lurk in the minds of many humans."

"No worries, Garnet. There is no need to apologize. We have all had ample opportunities to make mistakes on the Earth plane—it is all part of the learning process and the way we evolve as souls."

I hugged Martha good-bye and watched her disappear into the city. I looked cautiously at Albert, expecting him to give me a tongue lashing about judging other people, and he did not disappoint.

"If you truly love other people, as you should, you will not judge them for what they say or do. The Source does not judge humans for their actions on Earth and nor should you. When you judge other humans you are assuming you know all the facts about them, but you never do. You can't possibly know all the things they have experienced and the emotions they have felt unless you had traveled with them every step of the way.

"Unconditional love means love without any strings attached and without expecting anything in return. It means loving someone without reservations or judgment, regardless of what they may have done in the past. It is the kind of love humans should aspire to project to everyone around them each and every day. Unconditional love is the only kind of love shared by souls on the Spirit Side, which makes this place so special. When you go back home remember what you learned here today, and strive to be a better person. Even one person can make a difference, and I challenge you to instigate the changes you want to see in your world."

I felt like a child being scolded for fighting at school. Albert was right, as always. He had thrown down the gauntlet—and now it was up to me to carry the torch of enlightenment back to Earth. After all, who was I to look down on people just because they happen to be gay or sell their bodies for money? They say people who live in glass houses shouldn't throw stones, and if anyone peered through my glass walls they would see a naked man pretending to be dressed in a tuxedo.

Albert announced it was time for me to return home for a spell so I could collect my thoughts before our next excursion. So I followed him out of the Spirit Side, eager to be going back home for a brief respite from my adventures. As we neared the Earth, I stopped momentarily to admire the stunning beauty of my planet as it floated in a sea of black ink dotted with millions and millions of stars. Viewing Earth from this perspective was a thrill very few humans have been able to enjoy. Too bad everyone couldn't see our planet like I was seeing it now—and then maybe they would view it as a precious jewel worthy of more respect.

I got back to my home without incident and once again slipped back into my slumbering body. I was mentally exhausted from all the new information I had to assimilate, so I welcomed the chance to return to my temporal life on Earth where I could recoup my energy. Albert promised to return in a few days to introduce me to some highly evolved souls on the Spirit Side who would regale me with startling revelations about their famous lives from the past. Despite my weariness, I could hardly wait for his return.

Chapter Eighteen
Phantom of the Mansion

Although I seldom watch television, I happened to catch the tail end of a show about a haunted house while I was waiting for Albert to return. It was a country manor in the Cotswold's in England that been built in the nineteenth century. The show was about a team of paranormal investigators who had been summoned by the owners of the mansion to determine if it was haunted by ghosts.

The husband and wife who resided there had moved in only six months before and had since been plagued by strange and unexplained occurrences. They had often heard footsteps coming from the second floor when no one else was in the house. Frequently, lights in the house would flick on and off by themselves and cupboard doors in the kitchen would open and slam shut on their own. And one night the man of the house had witnessed a floating ball of light moving toward him in his bedroom, disappearing just before it reached him.

This couple was understandably spooked by these events, and they wanted to get to the bottom of it all—which is why they hired the paranormal detectives. The show ended with the head investigator explaining that their instruments had detected a paranormal presence in the house, although they had not been able to witness any of the unusual activity the owners had encountered.

My curiosity was aroused by this show. I wondered if the paranormal activity had been caused by a human who had learned to utilize the power of focused thoughts to move matter, like the monk I had seen in northern India, or was it a spirit from beyond the veil trying to get their attention.

When Albert returned as promised, I asked him if he knew what could have caused the unusual happenings in that house in England.

Albert gave me a knowing smile when I posed the question to him.

"I wondered when you would get around to asking me about paranormal activity on Earth," he responded. "Let me take you to that house in England so you can see for yourself."

I eagerly trailed Albert as we whisked our way to jolly old England where I soon recognized the Cotswold's mansion featured in the television show. Albert said this house had been built by a wealthy merchant in the early 1800s. He had lived there happily for many years with his wife, Anne, and their three children. But the happy days came to an abrupt halt one day when the merchant was away on business. In the dead of night a burglar, who thought no one was at home, broke into the house to steal their valuables. Anne heard a noise on the main floor and went downstairs to investigate, surprising the thief who was dropping silverware into his knapsack. The culprit panicked when he saw the lady of the house and rushed toward her with his knife drawn. Poor Anne was stabbed several times before the burglar fled the house.

Anne died quickly, and her spirit left her body but lingered in the house in a state of confusion. Her soul did not immediately remember who it was or that it needed to transition to the Spirit Side, because its vision was clouded by the pain and anguish Anne had felt during her encounter with the thief. Anne's spirit did not want to leave her children behind, so she remained at the house to watch over them. Years went by and her children grew up and left home, but her soul still lingered at the house, waiting for them to return.

Anne's spirit caused the paranormal activities in the house because she wanted to frighten the occupants, hoping they would be scared away so her children could return to the house.

"Why doesn't Anne's soul transition to the Spirit Side? Doesn't she realize her children are following their own paths on Earth, and she will see them once again when they cross over themselves?" I asked.

"What has happened to Anne occurs infrequently. Her soul was temporarily hijacked by the strong emotions she felt just before she died, and it was not able to see the true picture about life on Earth. Her spirit guides have been doing their best to persuade Anne to follow them Home, but Anne's soul has ignored them so far. Her guides are content to wait until Anne's soul is ready to leave, because linear time does not exist on the Spirit Side, and a couple of hundred years on Earth is just the blink of an eye to them. And they know this confused spirit will eventually make the transition to the Spirit Side—because no one is ever lost or abandoned."

Albert led me into the house and up to the second floor. Standing at the end of the hallway was the shimmering outline of Anne's spirit, still dressed in her bloody nightgown. She held up her hand to stop our approach and called out to us in a shaky voice: "Halt. Who are you, and what do you want?"

Albert flashed one of his warm smiles and responded: "My name is Albert and this is the astral body of Garnet, who is still completing his journey on Earth. My friend wanted to see if ghosts were for real, so I brought him here to meet you. You may not realize it yet, but your physical body died tragically a long time ago, and you are hanging around this house instead of moving on to the Spirit Side. You are temporally stuck on the Earth plane, and you need to leave this place and cross over to your Home where your welcoming party is waiting with open arms."

"I don't know what you are talking about. I must stay here until my children return to this house so I can watch over them and protect them from harm. Please leave my house and take these squatters with you. I do not want them in my house."

At this point I noticed two other ethereal figures standing behind Anne. One was dressed in a Roman toga and the other was dressed in a satin floor-length evening gown. Albert advised that they were Anne's spirit guides who had stayed with her since her death, patiently waiting for Anne's soul to follow them to the Spirit Side. They moved closer to Anne and enveloped her in a warm astral hug, while sending a stream of unconditional love to infuse her body. Eventually Anne's wild-eyed look gave way to one of happy surrender, and she waved good-bye to us as she let herself be lifted up through the ceiling and into the night sky, on her way to the Spirit Side. It seemed Anne's soul had finally found its way Home with a little help from her friends.

Albert and I left the mansion to return to our roost high above our beautiful planet. Now I understood the truth about ghosts, and I felt good about the end result for Anne's grief-stricken soul. She was now in the warm embrace of her welcoming party, thanks to the loving guidance from her spirit guides. As Albert had told me many times before, no soul is ever forgotten or abandoned. We always return to the bliss of the Spirit Side no matter what we did or how we died on Earth.

We left England and journeyed to a small park near the outer fringe of Aglaia. I noticed a group of men gathered around a tall bearded man standing next to the small fish pond in the center of the plaza. When we got closer my heart skipped a beat as I recognized the man in the center—it was Jesus Christ.

Chapter Nineteen
Mother of God

I was delighted to see Jesus again. He was a noble soul who was very humble, considering the impact he has had on humans on Earth. I thought he must be a Master (or even further up the evolutionary ladder), although he had declined to comment when I had raised the question with him during our first meeting.

Jesus introduced me to men in his group, who were all dressed in the attire common to Jewish men in Palestine when Christ walked the Earth. They were the souls of his apostles who gathered here often to discuss the developments of the Christian Church since the early years. I listened to their conversation with great interest, fascinated by the depth of their knowledge.

When the gathering dispersed, Jesus approached me with a smile that lit up his whole face. "Come with me, I want you to meet someone special," he said.

Jesus led me toward the far edge of the park that was lined with benches. I noticed a woman sitting all alone on one of the benches, wearing garb common to Jewish women in the time of Christ. She smiled as we approached and extended her hand to me in greeting, as Jesus made the introduction.

"I want you to meet my mother, Mary. She is a special soul who has worked behind the scenes for centuries to help humans on their path to spiritual enlightenment. And she was a great mother for me during my life on Earth," Jesus said proudly. "I will leave you two to chat as I must meet with a group of souls who recently crossed over from Earth. They were all on a plane that crashed, killing over two hundred people." Jesus left the park, and I began the conversation with Mary.

"I am honored to meet you, Mary. When I was a child my mother always held you in high esteem. She prayed to you often, hoping you would intercede with Jesus to answer her prayers."

"I met your mother after she crossed over. We have had several pleasant chats; she is a kind and loving soul. All souls who have been mothers on Earth have a special bond that continues after we have returned to the Spirit Side."

"Much has been written about you, Mary, in the gospels and subsequently by the leaders of the Catholic Church. Is it all true, or did they make some of it up to embellish your image?" I ventured.

"As it is with most of the things described in the Bible and other scriptures, some of it is true but parts are pure fiction. It is true I gave birth to Jesus, but his conception happened in the normal course for women on Earth. I was not a virgin when Jesus was born, despite the position of the Church in this regard. I was married to Joseph, and we had intercourse regularly like all the other Jewish couples at the time. You have to remember that Joseph and I were not Christians—we were Jews who followed all the Hebrew laws and traditions of the time just as our parents did. And it would have been contrary to our laws for me to withhold sex from Joseph or vice versa.

"Jesus was conceived with the union of my husband's sperm and one of my eggs. I expected Jesus to be a special person because I had vivid dreams before he was born depicting him as the Messiah."

"Why does the Church assert you were a virgin when Jesus was born, and you were impregnated by the Holy Spirit?" I wondered.

"They had two reasons for creating this belief. The first had to do with the status of Jesus as the son of God. In an effort to embellish the story of Jesus with some pizzazz, they decided Jesus's conception had to have been a miraculous event, something out of the ordinary. So they came up with the story that the Holy Spirit, being a member of the Trinity, caused the conception of Jesus in my womb. This supported their assertion that Jesus was no ordinary man, but was the son of God. To close the circle on this belief, they had to emphasize I was a virgin and therefore the conception did not occur in the ordinary course between Joseph and me.

"The second reason has to do with the Church's distorted view on sexuality. Judaism encourages sex between a husband and wife as a way of bonding, even if it is for pleasure only and not for the purposes of procreation. They view sex as an essential part of a healthy and happy marriage. The Catholic Church, on the other hand, preaches that all forms of sexual activity are sinful except coitus between a husband and wife for the purpose of conceiving a child. It stems from their historical view that sex makes a person unholy and unclean, and sexual intercourse to produce children is just a necessary evil that cannot be avoided.

"Thus to the Catholic Church, a person cannot be truly pure and holy if they have engaged in sex. Because I was the mother of Jesus I deserved a special status in their doctrines, someone to be venerated by the masses. And to complete the picture of my holiness they depicted me as a virgin. Not just a virgin when Jesus was born, but a virgin all my life. And in order to be consistent with this belief they had to deny I had any children after Jesus.

"The truth is I had four sons and two daughters after Jesus was born, and all of them were conceived in the normal course with the seed of Joseph. The original scriptures did mention the siblings of Jesus in several places, although most of these passages were deleted after the fact to preserve the story of my virginity.

"It is the same twisted logic that caused them to deny Jesus was married to Mary Magdalene and the father of his children. It is a pity these distortions have survived all these years. I don't regard my life on Earth as somehow denigrated by not being a perpetual virgin, and I know Jesus feels the same way about his life on Earth. Unfortunately, it is difficult for the Church leaders to change course and revisit the dogmas they have taught for centuries."

"What was Jesus like as a child? Did he seem to be extraordinary in any way?"

"Jesus was a very ordinary child, and there was nothing about him that would indicate he had a special mission in life. He was a good child who never got into trouble, and he worked hard with Joseph to learn the carpentry trade. He did not quarrel with his brothers and sisters and he respected his elders."

"I would like to ask you about the so-called 'lost years' in the life of Jesus, from the time he was twelve until he began his ministry at thirty," I continued. "The New Testament is silent about this period, and no one knows for sure what Jesus did during these eighteen years. Can you shed some light on this mystery?"

"I can tell you what went on in his life during this period, since I am very familiar with the details. For the first five years, Jesus worked as a carpenter with his father and his life was fairly uneventful. When he was seventeen he married his childhood sweetheart, Mary

Magdalene, and they left on a journey of exploration and enlightenment soon after the wedding. They traveled to a remote location in the mountains of Tibet where they met with a Buddhist monk called Choden. Jesus had learned about this man from a traveler who had passed through Nazareth when Jesus was fifteen.

"Choden had studied the ways of Buddha all of his life and was a strong proponent of deep meditation as a way to achieve oneness with the universe. Jesus was a quick study, and within two years he could meditate for several hours at a time. Choden also taught Jesus how to access parts of his brain humans don't normally use, which allowed Jesus to tap into different energy sources in the universe. When utilizing this energy, Jesus was able to convert mass on the Earth plane into other forms of mass or streams of energy. This was how Jesus performed his miracles during his public life.

"When Jesus was nineteen, he and Mary returned to Palestine to live among the Essenes. He continued his spiritual education in that community for several years before returning to Nazareth, where he and Mary started their family. When he was thirty Jesus began his public ministry, which has been described in the New Testament."

"Did you know your son would be crucified?" I asked Mary.

"Jesus had a premonition about his crucifixion, and he warned me about it. He said his death on the cross was necessary and unavoidable, and I was not to try to stop it in any way. He assured me his soul would live on and we would meet once again in Heaven after my death. He asked me to hide his children to ensure they would escape persecution, which I did. After his death I helped Mary Magdalene flee to another country with her children, where they lived normal lives in obscurity."

"Can you tell me where they lived after the death of Jesus and who their descendants are?" I asked hopefully.

"No, I am not at liberty to disclose that information because it would serve no useful purpose at this time," Mary responded. "You will be able to access this information when you cross over here yourself."

I was not surprised Mary would not reveal this information to me since Albert had previously declined to answer the very same question. Imagine what a commotion it would cause if this information became public. Everyone with a direct blood connection to Jesus would want to open a winery and try their hand at changing water into wine. Not to mention all the people who would drown trying to walk across the Mediterranean Sea. I could see why it was best to keep it a secret.

"Thank you for taking the time to meet with me today, Mary. I really enjoyed our conversation, and I hope we can do this again."

I gave Mary a hug and bade her farewell. Albert and I left the park and headed toward the main boulevard of the city.

"I am grateful to you, Albert, for arranging these meetings today. I was delighted to see Jesus again and meet with his apostles, and my meeting with Mary was totally enthralling. Are there any more secrets of the Catholic Church you can reveal to me?"

"There are many more, indeed, which you will be able to discover in good time. But I will take you to meet a modern-day disciple of Christ—a pope who was murdered shortly after his investiture."

Chapter Twenty
Vatican Intrigue

Albert and I strolled down the main boulevard of Aglaia, weaving our way through the crowd. We entered the main plaza of the city and turned into a small side street to the left of the water fountain. After several blocks the street curved to the right and dead-ended at a small park filled with oak trees and colorful flowers in bloom. In the center of the park beside the small fish pond I noticed an elderly man sitting alone on a wooden bench. He wore a white cassock with a gold crucifix hanging from a chain around his neck. He reminded me of someone I had seen in a newscast many years ago, although I could not put my finger on it.

We sat down on a nearby bench, and Albert made the introduction. "Garnet, I would like to introduce you to Albino Luciani. In his most recent incarnation on Earth he was best known to the world as Pope John Paul I."

I shook the pontiff's hand without saying a word. I remembered now why his face looked familiar—he had been elected Pope in 1978 but died only thirty-three days later under what many claimed to be suspicious circumstances.

"A pleasure to meet you, Garnet," John Paul said as he grasped my hand firmly. "You are no doubt wondering why Albert brought you here to meet with me, so let me explain the purpose of this visit.

"I understand from Albert you have agreed to be his messenger on Earth so his revelations would be available to everyone. And to this end, you have written two books and are working on the third. I also know you were raised as a Roman Catholic, although you no longer go to church because you have many doubts about the rules and beliefs of the Church. You have been critical of the Church and its hierarchy, suggesting its religious leaders are a group of out-of-touch old men who continue to adhere to the centuries-old strategy of controlling the masses through guilt and fear.

"I did not ask for this meeting so I could chastise you for your blasphemy, because I agree with your observations. You may be surprised at this, but you must realize I am now back on the Spirit Side where I can fully understand the reality of life on Earth and the role organized religions have played in human civilization.

"As you have noted, the Church began as a venue to propagate the teachings of Jesus Christ, a worthy endeavor indeed. Unfortunately, it got hijacked along the way by men who shaped it to serve their own earthly agendas. They developed its rules and beliefs as a way to satisfy their desire for power and control, which has caused a lot of pain and suffering over the centuries.

"And it is unfortunate that even in the twenty-first century the leadership of the Church still stumbles about blindly enforcing rules that no longer make any sense in modern civilization. It is true most men do not like change, and it is especially true in the case of old men. And the Pope and the cardinals clearly seem to have the mindset of old men who want to preserve the status quo at all costs, regardless of the wishes of their followers.

"In my last incarnation, I saw firsthand how this doctrinal intransigence could get out of control. I died only thirty-three days after I became Pope because I was murdered by a group of Vatican insiders who were fearful I would introduce reforms that would strike at the heart of the Church and its beliefs. They were so vehemently opposed to my plans that they panicked and hired an assassin to poison me before I could implement my changes."

"So who were the people who arranged your death?" I blurted out, unmindful I had interrupted his story.

"I now know who they were, but it would serve no useful purpose to disclose this to you. These men have all crossed over to the Spirit Side themselves, and I have forgiven them for their crime. I understand the reality of life on Earth, and I love them all unconditionally the same as I love all other souls."

"What were the radical reforms you had proposed?" I continued.

"The major reform related to the Church's policy on birth control. I firmly believed the prohibition on the so-called artificial birth control, such as the use of the pill, condoms, IUDs and the like, was very outdated and not in step with the mores of modern society. I was adamant this policy should be rescinded, and I let my views be known as soon as I was elected Pope. Many cardinals were aghast at the prospect, since it would be contrary to the Church's long-held belief that the Pope was infallible because his pronouncements came directly from God, and God could never be wrong. If I repealed the rule about birth control, they reasoned, it would mean all the previous Popes who had supported the policy would then be wrong, and this was not possible.

"What they failed to consider was the notion that God, who is all powerful and without limitations, could change his mind from time to time. So an easy and logical explanation for the change to the birth control policy was that the earlier Popes were right when they supported the policy, but I would also have been right when I repealed the policy because God, in his infinite wisdom, had changed his mind.

"My argument, for the most part, fell on deaf ears. And when they realized I was not going to change my plans, the perpetrators took matters into their hands before it was too late to stop me.

"I am telling you this story because you have assailed the Church's birth control policy in your books, and I wanted you to know a lot of other Catholics, including a former Pope, concur with your position. Hopefully this policy, which is ignored by a great many practicing Catholics, will be repealed some day."

"Thank you for being so candid with me, Your Holiness. With your permission, I will share your story in one of my books."

"By all means, tell the world about our meeting and what I have revealed to you. Be forewarned, however, because the cardinals will scoff at your story, as will many rank-and-file Catholics. Humans tend to believe only the things they want to believe, and they are reluctant to entertain ideas that run contrary to their own belief systems. This is especially true when it comes to religion."

John Paul stood up to leave, and I shook his hand in farewell. I watched him disappear around the street corner, wondering how things would be different on Earth if he hadn't been murdered.

"John Paul's demise at the hands of those culprits in the Vatican was despicable conduct," I said to Albert, "and something I never could have imagined to be possible. I had always been taught that the men who ran the Church were all devoted to the teachings of Jesus."

"As I told you before," Albert responded, "the religious leaders of the Church are humans who are subject to negative emotions like everyone else. They have their own agendas and some of them will go to great lengths to ensure their vision for the Church will be fulfilled.

"To better demonstrate this point, I think it would be useful for you to meet another disciple of Jesus who strayed way off course and did some loathsome things to innocent young children."

Chapter Twenty-One
Uncontrollable Urges

I waited quietly on the bench beside Albert, enjoying the sweet fragrance wafting up from the lilies in the flowerbeds. I was in no rush to leave because the ambiance in the little park was delightful, and I wanted some quiet time to reflect on my recent meetings.

My daydreaming was interrupted when we were approached by a tall thin man wearing a black suit and a white roman collar, looking very much like the Catholic priests I remembered from my youth. His lips were pulled back in a wry grin, and his handshake was firm, as Albert made the introductions: "I would like to introduce you to Patrick, who was a Roman Catholic priest in Ireland in his most recent life on Earth. Since you were raised as a Roman Catholic, I thought you might find his story interesting."

"Top of the morning to you, Garnet. I know your ancestors on your mother's side came from Ireland, so the story of my last life may be of special interest to you. Ireland is a wonderful country resplendent with lush green vegetation and plagued by mischievous leprechauns. And it is the only place on Earth where every Tom, Dick, and Harry is named Patrick.

"I enjoyed my last life there very much, until my wheels fell off the rails.

"I was born right after the end of the Second World War to my working-class parents in Dublin. My family was not well off by any means, although we always had a roof over our heads and food on the table. I was the youngest of four children, with an older brother and two older sisters. We were a close-knit family that enjoyed picnics in the park and jovial family dinners where the conversation was always lively.

"My early life, for the most part, revolved around school and the Church. My family was very religious and we attended holy mass every Sunday at the nearby Catholic Church, not to mention on all the Holy

Days of Obligation and a smattering of other occasions throughout the year.

"Religion was an important part of our family life, and we followed all of its rules faithfully and without question. Despite their religious fervor, my parents enjoyed Irish wit and humor even when it touched on themes that should have been sacrosanct. My mother often repeated a facetious prayer she had learned from her mother: 'When you pass from this world, may you get to Heaven a half hour before the devil knows you're dead.'

"Like my older brother and many other good Catholic boys, I served mass as an altar boy for our parish priest, a doddering older man who was a stickler for details. In those days mass was conducted in Latin, and all the altar boys had to memorize Latin prayers that were recited with the priest at every service. At the time I didn't know what the prayers meant, but that didn't bother me as long as I could pronounce the words correctly to avoid censure by the priest.

"In high school I was like most other red-blooded Irish boys—sneaking in a pint of Guinness here and there and chasing the pretty girls in the school. Despite my raging hormones, I could never even get to first base with any of my dates—such were the mores of the times—although it was not from a lack of trying.

"And then in my senior year of high school we got a new parish priest—Father O'Neill. He was young, dynamic, and full of life, and he could easily relate to the teenagers in the parish. I was captivated by his charisma, and I began to look up to him as my role model. Before I knew it was happening, I started to imagine myself as a priest like Father O'Neill. This seed took hold and continued to grow and, after several heart-to-heart talks with Father O'Neill, I decided I would like to try the priesthood.

"My mother was ecstatic when I broke the news—she would not have been any happier if she had won the lottery. So with the blessings of my family I entered the seminary at Holy Cross College when I finished high school.

"When I graduated from the seminary, I was inducted into the priesthood and assigned to a parish in Dublin as an assistant to the parish priest. After a couple of years there to learn my trade, my bishop asked me to become the pastor in a rural parish south of Dublin. I was delighted to take the assignment, and I soon found myself immersed in my new posting, which I thoroughly enjoyed.

"After a couple of years at the parish, I became anxious and uneasy. I was a heterosexual young man with very active hormones, but the Church dictated that I had to remain celibate for my whole life. Because of this policy, I had no outlet for my surging sexual drive, which bottled up inside me until I felt I was going to burst.

"Until finally one day I succumbed to the dark side. I began to lure a few of my younger altar boys to my rectory where I would fondle them in my bedroom. I loathed myself for doing this, but I couldn't seem to stop myself, try as I might.

"I managed to get away with this despicable conduct for a long time, mainly because I threatened the children into silence. I told them God would severely punish them and their families if they ever told anyone what I had done. And since parish priests were all held in high esteem in those days, these boys also sensed that their parents would not have believed them if they had broken their silence.

"And then one day, to my surprise, I was summoned for a meeting with my bishop in Dublin, who revealed he had received a complaint about me from a couple in my parish. They had told my bishop I had sexually abused their little boy. My bishop had listened politely and then warned them against believing this outrageous story. He said I was a fine upstanding member of his clergy and it would be unthinkable for me to have done such a thing. Because bishops were held in even higher regard than priests, he managed to convince them their son had a vivid imagination, and it would be very detrimental to the Church if they spoke to anyone else about this matter.

"When the bishop asked me if there was any truth to the allegation, I broke down and confessed everything. I promised I would never do it again and begged him for another chance. He agreed to give me an opportunity to redeem myself, and he transferred me to another rural parish west of Dublin.

"At first I was true to my word at my new parish, but I soon slid back into the depths of depravity. The cycle repeated at this parish and two more after that. My bishop thought he could sweep the problem under the rug by shuffling me around the diocese, but it didn't work. He was very careful to ensure the civilian authorities were never notified of my transgressions, because it would have been scandalous for the Church. He always seemed to put the reputation of the Church ahead of the welfare of the children of his diocese.

"At long last my bishop threw in the towel and removed me from parish life. He assigned me to a desk job in the diocese headquarters where I had no contact with children. I stayed there until I died from a stroke in my early sixties.

"I am thoroughly ashamed of my conduct in that life. What I did to those children was inexcusable, and I have spent much of my time since I crossed over trying to understand what went wrong. There is no doubt in my mind that the root cause of my perversion was the Church's policy on celibacy. It is simply unhealthy and unnatural to deny priests the right to marry and enjoy a consensual outlet for their sexual energy. The numerous instances of priestly abuse of children that have come to light in recent times bear witness to the tragic effects of this wrong-headed policy.

"I have spoken to a number of former priests here on the Spirit Side, some of whom abused children themselves, and they all agree celibacy serves no useful purpose and has caused a lot of pain and suffering over the years. The Church has always been run by a bunch of old men who do not like change, and changing the celibacy policy would constitute an earth-shattering event for most of them. Many former Catholic priests on the Spirit Side plan to return to Earth at some point in an effort to make changes to this rule. Time will tell whether this will work."

"Did you plan any of this abuse in your Life Plan, Patrick, or was it just another case of free will running amok?" I asked when he had paused for breath.

"I did not plan the abuse in my Life Plan, although I did plan on circumstances that would entice me to join the priesthood. I also knew at the time I would be subject to powerful sexual urges after I became a priest, but I thought I would be strong enough to resist. Now that I look back on it, I was not yet ready as a soul for such a challenge and I should have deferred this test to a later life."

"Thank you for being so candid with me, Patrick. With your permission I will tell your story to the world. Maybe someday the Church hierarchy will see the light and change their policy," I said as Patrick stood up to leave. I could see he had a lot on his mind, and he would no doubt be planning a return to the Earth plane to make amends.

Albert and I retraced our steps back to the main city plaza, where I noticed a crowd gathered in front of a small stage at the far end of the square. On the stage were five lithe young women wearing short skirts and patent leather dancing shoes, while behind them a merry band of fiddlers delighted the onlookers with a traditional Irish hornpipe. The dancers were doing an Irish step dance in perfect synchronization, keeping their upper bodies stiff and their arms straight at their sides. The intricate footwork, the rhythmic clicking of their shoes, and the toe-tapping music was mesmerizing. It was like a performance from *Riverdance*.

When the dance was finished the young performers went out into the crowd to fetch volunteers for a dance lesson. To my surprise, a pretty young lass snared my hand and pulled me up on the stage, along with four other lucky fellows. They began by showing us a few very simple dance steps that seemed easy enough, at least until the music began. The fiddlers launched into another lively hornpipe as the students valiantly tried to keep up.

I felt awkward at first, but then I got the hang of it as the cadence of the music infused me with the urge to gyrate my whole body in time to the music. My feet seemed to move on their own, without any direction from me, and I sensed I had tapped into a residual memory of a previous life in Ireland. Dancing had never felt so good—and I didn't want it to end.

After several minutes of exuberant frolicking the music stopped. I left the stage reluctantly, hoping they would ask me to join their troupe. Instead, they smiled and bade me good-bye, putting an end to my budding dance career. I found Albert in the crowd, and I wondered what he thought about my performance.

Albert gave me a wink and one of his Cheshire cat grins. I could tell he had enjoyed it almost as much as I had.

"You did not do badly for someone with two left feet," Albert opined. "If you keep practicing someday you will be able to walk and chew gum at the same time."

I feigned a frown at Albert, as I was getting used to his humor (or lack thereof). Not even Albert's wisecracks could wipe the smile off my face.

As the crowd dispersed, we sat down at one of the tables, with Albert in silent contemplation. I did not want to interrupt his thoughts, so I waited quietly for him to announce our next destination. When Albert's silence dragged on for what seemed like an inordinate length of time, I could no longer restrain myself, and I tugged at Albert's arm to get his attention.

"Before we continue our journey in search of wisdom, Albert, I would like to ask you a question that has been on my mind ever since we first met on that fateful day in 2007. It relates to something you told me about free will and my soul's right to choose when to leave this incarnation.

"You said we all have free will to make decisions and take actions on Earth, and we are not allowed to remember what we put in our Life Plans before we were born. Because of this you stated it was very likely we would stray off our intended path often during our lives, sometimes in very significant deviations. You also asserted that no one dies by accident since our souls have the unfettered right to decide when to leave an incarnation.

"At the time, I was skeptical about how it was possible for my soul to choose my time of death when all the people I interact with every day—on the streets and highways, at work and at play—are exercising their free will without knowing what my soul has in mind for me. It seemed likely the everyday clash of these free-will actions would result in events and consequences that could not be foreseen by my soul, and I might die in an accident before my soul was ready to leave.

"But you had a ready response to my dilemma—a solution that made sense and tied up the loose ends in your revelation. You said my guardian angels were always present to ensure my physical life would not end before my soul was ready to exit. My guardian angels would intervene whenever necessary to prevent my untimely death, often in situations where I would be totally unaware they had acted to save me.

"I would like to meet one of my guardian angels, Albert, so I can extend my gratitude for a job well done. Can you arrange a meeting?"

"No problem," Albert said and nodded with a smile. "Follow me and I will introduce you to Anapiel, who has been watching over you since birth."

Chapter Twenty-Two

Angels on Call

Albert and I headed back to the main street of Aglaia, where we ambled among the throngs of souls until we reached the front of a majestic edifice with stunning white marble pillars and gold angel-wing inlays dispersed randomly in its polished façade. Albert pointed out that this was the Hall of Angels—a place for angels to hang out and socialize. Just inside the massive front door was a large lobby with a magnificent crystal chandelier that sparkled from the light streaming in through the skylights. The high domed ceiling was adorned with murals of angels that looked like they could have been painted by Michelangelo.

We walked toward a solitary figure seated on a wing-back chair covered with blue and gold brocade. She was the most beautiful woman I had ever seen, with long, silky black hair, radiant blue eyes, and a peaches-and-cream complexion. She was wearing a white silk sari, white satin slippers, and a smile that could launch a thousand ships. And contrary to my expectations, she did not have wings sprouting from her shoulders.

Albert and I sat down on the sofa facing her chair. I didn't know if I should bow, kiss her hand, or ask for her autograph. So I sat there quietly, waiting for Albert to make the first move.

"Namaste, Anapiel. I brought Garnet here because he wanted to meet one of his guardian angels. He needs no introduction to you as you have been watching over him for many years now."

"Nice to meet you face to face, Garnet," Anapiel responded with a voice sweeter than a chorus of songbirds at sunrise. "How can I help you?"

"The pleasure is all mine, Anapiel. How did you come to be my guardian angel and what exactly do you do in this role?"

"When a spirit decides to incarnate, the Council of Wise Ones asks for volunteers to fill the role of guardian angel for that soul during its life on Earth. I offered my services before you were born, and now here I am. You also have two other guardian angels who volunteered just as I did.

"My duties as your guardian angel are fairly straightforward. My job is to ensure your physical body doesn't perish before your soul is ready to leave the incarnation. Your soul has the right to choose your time of death, although preserving this right is often a challenge. As you have noted, every human on Earth has free will to make decisions and take actions, and they must do so without the benefit of knowing what is in their Life Plans or in the Life Plans of anyone else. This constant clash of free will actions often leads to events that are not anticipated by your soul, which could result in your untimely death.

"This is where I come in. My job is to manipulate the circumstances and events in your life so you do not become the victim of an accidental death before your time is up. I can employ several methods to accomplish this goal.

"Sometimes I will send you a strong intuitive message to encourage you to take an action or refrain from doing something. If I foresee you will be involved in a car accident on your way to work, I might send you a message to take a different route to work. You would have a sudden hunch you should take a different route to your office, although you would have no idea where the thought came from. If you ignored my suggestion and proceeded on your usual route I would have to take other actions, like causing your tire to go flat or your engine to stall. If necessary, I could physically manipulate the vehicles at the crucial intersection to ensure you narrowly missed the collision. You would not be aware of any of this, but you might thank your lucky stars you missed a horrible collision by only a few seconds.

"I use my power to manipulate events in your life only to prevent an early death, or an injury serious enough to totally derail you from the path you laid out in your Life Plan. I will not interfere to keep you on track if your free-will actions would take you off course, because that would defeat the whole purpose of your journey on Earth. Staying on course is one of the challenges you face as a human, and we cannot interfere to make things easier for you."

"You must not have been very busy with my life so far," I replied. "I don't recall any near misses that could have ended my life."

"Of course you don't, because I don't send you a report every time it happens. I saved your butt so many times that I lost count. Let me give you a few examples of my intervention.

"Do you remember the time when you were five and visiting your grandmother in the city? You were playing catch in her front yard when the ball got away and rolled out onto the street. You ran between parked cars, without looking, to fetch your ball, and the driver of the car motoring by had to slam on his brakes to avoid hitting you. The car skidded to halt inches from your foolish little body, and you were not injured. Well, guess who pushed the car to a stop before it reached you?

"And then there was the time when you were sixteen and returning with your friends from a dance in the next town. The young driver recklessly tried to pass another vehicle on the narrow highway at a very high speed. He nearly lost control when he swerved too far to the left and his front wheel got caught up in the loose gravel on the shoulder. Had I not intervened to push the car back on the road, you would have died when the vehicle plunged into the ditch and rolled over.

"And do your recall that time when you were a young lawyer rushing to get to a meeting and foolishly decided to jaywalk across a busy street without looking both ways? You were almost run over by a speeding gravel truck in your haste, and I saved the day once again by causing your valise to slip out of your hands just before you left the sidewalk.

"I could go on and on, but I think you get the picture."

"Thank you, Anapiel, for all your interventions. I had no idea I had flirted with death so many times. Please keep up the good work.

"Now tell me something truthfully. If you are watching over me all the time, does this mean you are peeping at me when I am in the shower?"

"Hell no. Even though I enjoy a good laugh as much as the next person, I do have my boundaries. You can rest assured no one over here has any desire to see your naked body."

I could see that Anapiel and Albert were two peas from the same pod when it came to humor, so I decided to ignore her comment and ask a serious question.

"Because it is your job to make sure my soul has the right to choose the time of my death, can you tell me when I will exit from my life on Earth?"

"I know what your soul is planning right now, but I am not allowed to disclose this information to you. Besides, the exit date your soul has in mind is not etched in stone. Your soul can change this date as your life progresses, and this decision is based on its assessment of the events it has encountered so far compared to what it had hoped to accomplish before you were born. So your exit point is a moving target with your soul at the controls."

"I expected this answer from you," I responded, "and I am actually thankful you can't tell me when I will die. Can you tell me more about who you are? Have you ever incarnated on Earth?"

"I am an angel—a special spirit created to help the Wise Ones oversee and regulate the incarnations on Earth. Like you, I am an individual aspect of the Source connected to everyone and everything in the universe. I am a highly evolved energy being who does not need to experience life on the denser planes in order to advance my evolution, which is why I have not incarnated on Earth. Some angels do choose to incarnate on Earth to help other souls with their journeys. And sometimes Earth angels will materialize a physical body on Earth when necessary to help people in trouble.

"It is my great joy to watch over you and protect you from accidents whenever it is necessary. I have been doing this for a long time, and I never get tired or bored. There is always something new and exciting happening on your plane, which keeps me on my toes.

"Now if you will excuse me, I must be off. One of the other humans I watch over is soon to be in need of a little help. Farewell for now, and we can chat again when you cross over to the Spirit Side."

Anapiel rose from her chair and floated out of the room, looking back once to wave good-bye. Albert led me out of the Hall of Angels and onto the main boulevard. When we reached the main plaza we sat down at one of the tables near the fountain to enjoy a jazz choral group who was thrilling the audience with a very ebullient version of "Mack the Knife."

After the ensemble finished their set I expected Albert to take me to our next destination, but he didn't seem to be in any hurry. I soon found out why we had lingered in the square. A distinguished elderly gentleman, decked out in a spiffy three-piece suit, strolled toward us and sat down at our table.

"Good day, Sir Arthur," Albert greeted the man. "Thank you for joining us today."

"It is my pleasure," the gentleman responded in a dignified voice.

"Garnet, I would like you to meet Sir Arthur Conan Doyle, who was an accomplished and prolific writer during his last life on Earth. You may remember him as the author of the Sherlock Holmes books."

I rose to shake his hand, thrilled at the chance to meet such a famous writer.

"I wanted you to meet Sir Arthur because he is one of your writing coaches. He has helped you in many ways since you began writing your books, and he has promised to be there for you in the future."

"It is an honor to meet you, Sir Arthur. I didn't realize I had a writing coach."

Sir Arthur gave me a knowing smile and responded with a twinkle in his eyes: "All writers on Earth have one or more writing coaches, although most are not aware of this arrangement. When you were developing your Life Plan for your current life, I volunteered to be your coach because I liked what I had seen of your prose in some earlier lives, and I thought you had potential. I am satisfied so far that my optimism has not been misplaced, even though I wish you would pay more attention to the thoughts I send to you when you are writing. You pick up most of my messages, but you still miss some important intimations."

"What kind of messages do you send me?" I wondered.

"In your books you describe your conversations and astral adventures with Albert based on your memories of these encounters. Remembering these events is the easy part of writing your books. The bigger challenge is being able to describe what you saw in a way that clearly conveys the picture to the reader, using grammatically correct English. Your prose must be interesting, entertaining, and easy to understand in order to impact the greatest number of readers. Albert's revelations are intended to provide inspiration and comfort to humans searching for meaning in their lives, and it is up to you to deliver his messages with eloquence.

"When you are struggling to describe your adventures with Albert, I do my best to send you intuitive flashes of thought to inspire you to create prose that will do justice to the truths revealed by Albert. So when a brilliant idea pops into your head as you write, you now know you didn't generate it yourself—it actually came from your friends beyond the veil. And please understand this is not something unique in your situation. All writers on Earth have writing coaches on the Spirit Side to enhance their creative talent in very subtle ways, even though most would deny it."

"Now I understand where my ideas come from, thank you for your help. But is there any way you can send your messages to me in a more direct route, like my communications with Albert?"

"No such luck, I'm afraid. You will have to play by the rules like all the other authors. Except you now have one advantage the others don't have—you understand I will be sending you my thoughts and advice as you write, and you will be listening with keen interest."

"Why can't you dictate my manuscripts to me, word for word? It would make everything so much easier."

"I think you already know the answer to this question. I am not here to do your work for you. You must do things the hard way, because this is the only way for you to grow and evolve. You knew about the writing challenges you would encounter before you incarnated, so suck it up and quit your whining. I can only go so far with my assistance, and it is up to you to carry the ball the rest of the way into the end zone."

"Fair enough, Sir Arthur. From now on I will listen carefully for your messages, so keep them coming."

Sir Arthur got up to leave, and I shook his hand in farewell. I glanced at Albert to see if he had arranged any more meetings, but he gave me an inscrutable smile. So I sat back down and waited patiently for his next move.

I was thrilled to meet one of my guardian angels and my writing coach, although there was still a missing piece to my team on the Spirit Side. Not long after we first met, Albert had told me I had two other spirit guides besides him, but he had refused to divulge their names or provide an introduction. So I thought I would try one more time.

"Albert, I am still curious about the identities of my other spirit guides. You have introduced me to many different souls on the Spirit

Side, but so far I have yet to meet any of my other guides. Is there any chance I can meet at least one of them before we leave?"

"I think you deserve that opportunity," Albert conceded. "Come with me and I will introduce you to one of the new members of your spirit guide team."

Chapter Twenty-Three
Guidance from Beyond the Veil

We ambled down the main boulevard of Aglaia for several blocks before turning right onto a narrow side street, eventually reaching a small plaza filled with tables and chairs. We made our way to a table near the water feature and sat down beside a Native American woman wearing a fringed buckskin dress and moccasins. She was very pretty, with expressive brown eyes and shiny black hair tied in a ponytail. Her perfect white teeth gleamed in the sunlight as she gave us a welcoming smile. She was slim and fit and looked to be in her mid-twenties.

"I would like you to meet Elina, one of your spirit guides who has been on your team for only a few years," Albert began.

"It's a pleasure to meet you, Elina," I said as I shook her hand. "Can you tell me more about yourself and how you came to be one of my spirit guides?"

"I am using the name I had in my last incarnation on Earth when I was a member of the Cheyenne tribe. I was a niece of Chief Black Kettle who was the chief of our band in southeastern Colorado Territory in the mid-eighteen hundreds. I was killed in 1864 in the Sand Creek Massacre when the Colorado Militia attacked our peaceful encampment without provocation. Most of our warriors were out hunting at the time, and we had no way to defend ourselves. They massacred over a hundred and fifty of my people, mostly women and children.

"Because of the violent nature of my death I had to spend some time in the reentry hospital here in Aglaia. However, now I am fully transitioned back to the Spirit Side and ready to continue with my evolution. The Council of Wise Ones recommended I spend time acting as a spirit guide before jumping back into another life on Earth. So when an opening came up in your spirit guide team, I volunteered. I have been one of your spirit guides ever since 2008, when you retired from your law practice."

"So what made you choose my spirit guide team?"

"We have known each other for a long time, even though you will not remember the details until after you cross over to the Spirit Side yourself. We have lived many lives together on Earth, and I wanted to help you in your current incarnation to pay you back for all the help you have given me in the past. This is how things work in the Spirit Side; we take great pride in helping other souls with their incarnations, which also aids in our own growth and evolution. Earth is a very tough school, and all the brave souls who choose to incarnate on your planet are grateful for any assistance we can provide from the Spirit Side.

"As Albert has revealed to you, spirit guides act as life coaches for the souls incarnated on Earth. Everyone has a least two or three guides, and they often change as one's life progresses. The guidance you needed most when you retired was much different from the guidance that was appropriate when you were in your twenties. The souls who volunteer to be spirit guides all have different backgrounds and talents because of their previous lives on Earth. The Wise Ones try to find volunteers whose previous life experiences will equip them with the wisdom and understanding required to best serve the needs of the souls who are having physical journeys on Earth.

"For the most part, spirit guides are not afforded the luxury of having direct telepathic contact with the humans they coach. Your contact with Albert is an exception that is used for a very specific purpose—to give Albert a venue for his revelations to be propagated to the masses. It was always the plan you would be Albert's messenger on Earth, but it was not intended to make your life any easier. Albert has not provided you with any direct insights that helped you decide which path to take when you reached a fork in the road. For guidance on those decisions, you have had to listen to the subtle messages from your other guides.

"As you know, your guides are constantly sending you messages to help you find the path you need to follow. This guidance might come in the form of an intuitive hunch, a soft whisper in your mind, a gut feeling, or a coincidental event. The difficult part for you, and for all other humans, is to recognize the messages and understand what they mean for you. This sounds easy enough, but it is hard to achieve because your mind is always so cluttered with thoughts about the past and the future that you miss a lot of our guidance. This is all part of the challenge of having a journey on Earth—a challenge you knowingly accepted before you chose to incarnate.

"I came on board when you retired from the law because we saw an opportunity at that time to make a better connection with you. We had a lot of difficulty getting through to you while you were practicing law because of the heavy stress load you were carrying. With that out of the way, we hoped you would become a better listener. And I joined your team since I had a lot of experience coaching people to be better listeners.

"Your ability to hear us has improved a great deal since 2008, although you still have a long way to go. This is why I agreed to meet with you today. I am hopeful you will leave this meeting with a renewed determination to hone your listening skills."

"Thank you for agreeing to be one of my coaches, Elina. What advice can you give me today to help me become a better listener?"

"Never dwell on the past. Everything you have already said or done in your life is water under the bridge. The past cannot be changed, and it should never be relived. Learn from the mistakes you have made and then move on. Regret is a very useless emotion that serves only to drain your energy in a whirlpool of guilt.

"By the same token, do not worry about the future. The universe will always unfold as it should, and you can never become lost in the abyss of our infinite cosmos. No matter what you do in this life you will always return Home where you will once again enjoy a blissful existence as an eternal being of energy. Your life on Earth should be viewed as an exciting adventure, something to be relished as each day passes without any fear or apprehension about what may arise tomorrow.

"If you can do this and focus your mind on living in the present, you will be delighted with your enhanced ability to discern the messages from beyond the veil. Any time you are searching for an answer or struggling to make a decision, sit quietly in meditation and ask Elina for help. I will always send you the answer, and your challenge will be to recognize my response from the thousands of other thoughts that swirl around in your mind every day. You must tread with caution because even when you clearly discern my guidance your mind will often try to rationalize a different course of action. Follow your heart and don't let yourself be ruled by your mind."

"I accept your advice, Elina, and I resolve to work harder at becoming a better listener."

"Great. Now if you have time, I would like to show you something that may help you achieve your goal."

"I have all the time you want. I like it up here, and I know when our meeting is over Albert will take me back home to live another day on Earth. The Spirit Side is so much more pleasant, Elina, that I am reluctant to go back."

"I know how you feel, but the time you have left on Earth is just the blink of an eye by our standards. You still have a lot more to accomplish, so hang in there and learn to enjoy your adventure."

Elina stood up and grasped my hand, leading me out of the plaza. I had no idea where we were going, although I was happy to follow her wherever she went.

Elina led me down a quiet street in a part of Aglaia I had never seen before. At the end of the road we left the city through a small wrought-iron gate and emerged at the top of a long sloping hill covered with ivy. We took a cobblestone path down toward the shore of a placid blue lake filled with crystal-clear water. Behind the lake in the distance I could see a range of towering mountains, their snowy peaks glistening in the sunlight.

When we reached the shore, Elina motioned for me to follow her onto a small ferry boat anchored at the pier. The ferryman launched the boat toward a nearby tree-covered island, his long oars creaking softly as they glided through the water. When we reached the island, we jumped out into knee-deep water and waded onto the shore. The lake water was cool and refreshing, and I had to stifle my impulse to dive in and frolic like a child at summer camp.

Elina guided me to a brick walkway that led to a majestic stone house at the edge of the forest. The front was all glass right up to the top of its vaulted two-story ceiling, providing a stunning vista of the lake and the city skyline. We entered through the open doorway and sat down on a sofa in front of the massive stone fireplace. The crackling fire filled the room with warmth and the sweet scent of burning birch logs. I soaked up the wonderful ambience of the room, content to wait for Elina to reveal the purpose of our visit.

And then I saw her standing on the second-floor balcony—a regal lady with jet-black hair that formed a knot of curls at the back of her head, tied down with silver ribbons. Her smooth skin glowed softly from the sunlight streaming in through the windows. She wore a white silk peplos adorned with silver beads, which hugged her voluptuous body from her shoulders to her ankles. She slowly descended the wide marble stairway beside the fireplace and smiled as she approached us, a near perfect picture of grace and elegance.

I rose up immediately, enchanted by her breathtaking beauty, and waited for Elina to make the introduction.

"Garnet, I would like to introduce you to Athena, who is one of our wise old souls, a Master who has roamed the Earth for eons spreading love and sharing her wisdom wherever she went. She was worshiped in ancient Greece as the goddess of wisdom, courage, and inspiration, and her reputation on Earth was richly deserved. I thought you could benefit from her wisdom."

I bowed down to kiss her outstretched hand, which smelled of fresh lavender. I sensed I was in the presence of greatness, and I waited for Athena to speak.

"Greetings, Garnet. Welcome to my home. Elina has told me about your mission on Earth, and I would be delighted to help you any way I can," Athena said at last.

"Are you really a goddess?" I blurted out.

"No, not in the way you understand this term. I am a soul just like you—a being of energy who spun out from the Source eons ago. I have lived countless lives on Earth and on many other planets in the universe, and I am at a very advanced stage of evolution. As a Master I no longer need to incarnate on the denser planes, but I do appear on Earth from time to time to assist other souls who need extra help during troubled times.

"I did walk the Earth in ancient Greece, sometimes performing humanitarian feats they thought to be miracles even though I was just tapping into the energy of the universe the same as any other Master. As a result of these so-called miracles the citizens of Athens concluded I was a goddess.

"I have always enjoyed helping other souls make the most of their journeys on the denser planes. Is there anything I can do for you?"

I decided to take the plunge and ask for her help. "I am struggling with my inability to clearly discern all the messages I get from my guides when I am back in my human body. I want to find my true path in life so I can accomplish what I had intended in my Life Plan. And I don't want to waste the remainder of my life careening down the wrong road in a daze. Can you help me?"

Athena smiled knowingly, and responded: "You have the same hang-ups that plague most souls having a human incarnation. You are frustrated because you don't know for sure where you should be going, and you are fearful of taking a wrong turn or making a mistake. Think of your life as a vast labyrinth of paths with numerous twists and turns, except there are no dead ends and you will always be able to find your way out of the maze. You will enjoy valuable life experiences no matter which path you choose, even when you stray off the path you had planned before you were born. So you need to relax and enjoy life wherever it may take you.

"Of course you will encounter many difficulties and obstacles on your journey, which is all part and parcel of a human incarnation. It is important for you to learn to recognize the difference between an obstacle meant to be overcome and a brick wall at the end of a dead-end street. In the case of the former, it is usually designed to test your determination—to see if you can persevere in a difficult situation without giving up. When you come upon this kind of obstruction, you should dig down deep, push your way through, and savor the satisfaction that will flow from this victory.

"On the other hand, if you find yourself staring at a brick wall that is blocking your path there is nothing to be gained by crashing into the bricks in a senseless rage. If this happens, you need to back away gracefully and find another street to continue your journey. Brick walls are life's way of telling you that you need to change direction.

"The real challenge is learning to tell one from the other. My advice to you is to listen to your feelings and follow your heart. Your intuition is never wrong, but your mind often is. When facing obstacles you must strive to rein in the thoughts that charge around your mind like wild horses on the loose and focus your attention on the whispers from your guides. Your guides are always there for you, and they will not let you down.

"Unfortunately, there is no magic sword I can give you to slay the fears and uncertainties that often rear their ugly heads in your life. Whenever you are feeling off-balance or despondent, sit somewhere quietly by yourself and ask Elina for her help. She will always come to your rescue as long as you are willing to listen to her advice.

"And when you finish your current incarnation, drop by for a cup of tea, and you can tell me all about your adventures on Earth."

"Thank you for sharing your wisdom, Athena. I look forward to meeting with you again."

I rose and bowed deeply, and Athena stepped closer and wrapped her arms around me in a warm embrace. Elina and I left the house and boarded the ferry. I sat in quiet contemplation as the boat glided smoothly across the lake toward Aglaia, thankful I had the opportunity to meet such a wise spirit.

Elina led me back to the small plaza in the city where Albert was waiting for us. Elina winked at Albert and gave me a farewell hug before disappearing around a corner. Albert did not say a word as we sat there enjoying the ambiance of the plaza. His poker face was unreadable, as usual, so I waited patiently for his next move.

At long last he looked at me and broke the silence.

"You have often complained that life on Earth is difficult, even though I told you many times you chose your life before you were born. And you often forget you are not alone in your current journey, although it may seem like you are at times. This is why I introduced you to your guardian angel, your writing coach, and another of your spirit guides; I wanted you to take comfort from the knowledge that these wise spirits are always there to help you. Before I take you back to your home I think you should meet one more wise spirit who works diligently behind the scenes to stamp out wickedness on your planet.

"And you will be surprised to learn who he is because he has been mistakenly vilified by humans for centuries. His name is Lucifer."

Chapter Twenty-Four
Lucifer Revealed

We headed back to the Hall of Angels where we sat down on one of the sofas in the huge lobby to wait for Lucifer.

"I thought you told me Satan doesn't exist?" I said at last.

"Satan does not exist, but Lucifer does. Lucifer is an angel who has been badly maligned by some humans who claim he is a fallen angel who has succumbed to the dark side. Many humans believe Lucifer is synonymous with Satan, except this could not be further from the truth. He will be here shortly, and you will be able to see for yourself."

This piqued my curiosity as I anxiously glanced around the lobby, hoping to spot him. Albert sat there passively with a serene expression on his face, confident our guest would show up in due course.

Before long I noticed movement out of the corner of my eye. I turned to see someone entering the lobby from a door on the far right. He was a handsome man with jet-black curly hair and ivory skin. He wore a long white cassock cinched at the waist with a blue sash, and his feet were bare. He smiled warmly as he approached us, his flawless white teeth gleaming from the light streaming in from the skylight overhead.

"Good day, gentlemen. I am Lucifer, also known as the morning star. You look surprised at my appearance, Garnet. You no doubt expected a demonic creature with horns and a pointed tail. Sorry to disappoint you, but my devil costume is at the cleaners. I wanted it to look good for Halloween.

"It is true I have been linked to Satan by some humans; however, they don't know the facts. First of all, Satan doesn't exit. He was invented by religious leaders as a tool to whip the masses into line. They used the devil to instill fear into the hearts of their followers to ensure their rules were followed without question. It was just another way of cementing their hold on power.

"Somehow my name got tangled up with Satan's, and I was characterized as a fallen angel who was expelled from Heaven for trying to usurp God's authority. In reality I am still one of the Source's faithful servants, and I do not encourage or foster evil deeds in humans. To the contrary, my role is exactly the opposite; I work behind the scenes to discourage evil thoughts and actions on the Earth plane.

"I am not allowed to directly intervene to prevent wicked events, although I do my best to influence those humans who are contemplating evil deeds or who are in a position to stop others from doing so. I influence people by sending them strong subliminal messages to encourage them to act in accordance with my wishes. It doesn't always work, as you can tell from all the violence on your planet, but I am happy to report I have been successful in preventing many calamities over the years.

"And in those cases where I have been unsuccessful in preventing a catastrophe, I provide counseling to the perpetrators when their souls cross over to the Spirit Side. The people who were evil monsters on Earth always need extra help to deal with the crimes they committed on Earth, so I hold their hands during their Life Reviews to help them learn from their experience and move on."

"You have an interesting story, Lucifer," I said after a moment of silence. "I commend you for your good work, but I am curious about the disasters you have prevented in the past. Can you give me some examples?"

"I don't like to boast, but I will disclose several of my good deeds so you can tell other humans the truth about me. Maybe then they will stop defaming my good name and allow me to take my proper place with the other angels.

"I was instrumental in the abolishment of slavery in the United States. I worked tirelessly on President Lincoln for a number of years, with constant intuitive whispers and messages in his dreams, to give him the courage and conviction to take the steps he did to abolish slavery. I am thankful he did so with my encouragement, and his actions put a stop to one of the most heinous practices in the history of America.

"In the Second World War, I worked hard to prevent Hitler from developing and using the atomic bomb in the war. Despite the Third Reich's frantic desire to be the first to use a fission bomb, I subtly encouraged the physicists on their nuclear team to drag their feet on the development of their bomb. They knew thousands of lives would be lost if the bomb was deployed by the Nazis, and I made them feel right about their decision to hinder its progress. This time my intervention worked, and the rest is history.

"One of my most significant accomplishments so far happened in 1962 during the Cuban missile crisis. The Soviet leader, Nikita Khrushchev, was so incensed at the American naval blockade of Cuba that he was ready to push the button to start World War III. I had to work long and hard to get him to take a breather and back down from his belligerent stance. In the end it worked, and the world was saved from a nuclear catastrophe."

"Wow. I am impressed," I gushed. "The people on Earth are entitled to know about this, and I will make certain they hear your story. Maybe then they will stop calling you the devil."

We bade farewell to Lucifer and sauntered casually out of the city and into the bucolic splendor of the lush meadow outside Aglaia. The bright sky overhead glimmered with a stunning array of iridescent blue hues that made the blue sky of Earth seem rather ordinary. I inhaled the sweet perfume from the wildflowers lining the edge of the path, as I listened to the haunting melody of a bluebird perched high in an oak tree.

As we rounded a gentle bend in the road I noticed a small outdoor stadium off to the left, with wooden bleachers on either side filled with spectators. I veered toward the stadium to get a better look, and Albert reluctantly trundled along beside me. As I got closer I could see a sporting event in progress. There were two teams with eleven players each, wearing colorful uniforms that resembled the soccer attire worn on Earth. The field was laid out like a soccer field with a goal at each end guarded by a goalkeeper. Like a soccer game, the players tried to maneuver the ball into the opposing team's net.

There was one big difference, however; the players were not allowed to touch the ball with any part of their bodies, not even their feet. They had to move the ball using only the energy of their thoughts—a soccer game ruled by telekinesis. The ball was constantly in flight, rarely touching down, as the players strained to focus their thought energy on sending the ball into the other team's net. The pace was fast and furious as the ball zipped through the air from end to end, finally stopping at the back of one of the nets. The crowd roared its approval, delighted at the deftness of the slick scoring play. I loved the action and wanted to stay for the whole game, only I knew that was wishful thinking on my part.

As I expected, Albert did not let me linger for long as he grasped my hand to lead me out of the Spirit Side and back to my home. He said we were nearing the end of our current round of adventures, and then he would leave me alone for several months. Before he left he wanted to provide me with a pleasant surprise as a reward for following his agenda so faithfully. *Bring it on, Albert, I can hardly wait!*

Chapter Twenty-Five
The Black Hole

I awoke back in my bedroom with the morning sun streaming through the windows. The joyful chorus from the songbirds welcomed me back to another day on Earth. I vividly remembered the astral adventure I just had with Albert while my body was fast asleep. Life on Earth in a human body seemed so pedestrian compared to exploring the universe as a being of energy. My life on Earth was not only wearisome but often fraught with despair, as I tried to find meaning in my existence. Albert's entry into my life had changed many things, and I now know my purpose for being here, even though I am not privy to all the plans I had made before I was born.

I now had a much better understanding about the Source and the diverse nature of the universe it has created, with billions of stars and countless dimensions populated by innumerable life forms, all of which was almost beyond my human comprehension. *Was the universe really infinite?* I wondered. Like most humans I had a hard time grasping the concept of infinity. The idea of a universe without borders was counterintuitive to me, something that didn't make sense to someone living on Earth and observing the universe with human perception. On the other hand, if the universe did have a boundary, what lay beyond its borders?

Was it true, as some theoreticians have postulated, that the space-time continuum was curved, and if you traveled for long enough in a straight line you would eventually return to your starting point? I didn't know if there was an answer to these questions, and I hoped Albert might be able to shed light on this enigma.

So when Albert fetched me for my next out-of-body excursion, I was ready with my questions. Albert listened patiently as I prodded him for answers.

"Come with me," he said at last. "I want to show you something that may satisfy your curiosity about the universe."

Albert took my hand and pointed toward the center of our Milky Way galaxy. The stars disappeared momentarily and then reappeared in all of their glory. I could not see our sun or my home planet or any of the constellations that could be seen from Earth. Ahead of us was a ring of stars surrounding a black circle that was devoid of any light.

Albert said we were looking at a black hole in the center of our galaxy. Black holes were a locality in space with very dense mass, usually caused by the collapse of a star. This highly concentrated mass had such a strong gravitational pull that nothing, not even photons of light, could escape. Everything that passed within its event horizon was sucked into its powerful vortex like particles of dust into a vacuum cleaner, never to be seen again.

I looked at Albert nervously, wondering why he had brought me here. Despite my obvious trepidation, Albert nudged me toward the black hole, with our descent accelerating as we got closer. The black abyss loomed larger and larger until it completely filled my field of vision and I could no longer see the neighboring stars. I could not resist the relentless pull from the ominous black mass ahead of me, and I felt like a fly being engulfed by the gaping mouth of a ravenous frog.

And then I no longer felt any movement. I was suspended in a morass of complete darkness—with nary a flicker of light in any direction. I could not even see the ethereal outline of my physical body that I normally could see on my astral excursions. Albert had disappeared from sight, and I got no response when I called out to him. I could not see, feel, or sense anything around me, as if all of my sensory inputs had been shut down by some invisible force. I felt like a scintilla of consciousness floating in a vast ocean of nothingness.

Then I wondered if I really did exist—or was I just suffering from the grand delusion that I was an eternal being of energy. Maybe I was merely a character in a dream, and I would disappear forever when the dreamer awoke. Albert had told me I was an individual aspect of the Source connected to everything else in the universe. But in this black hole I felt totally isolated and not connected to anything.

Albert said there was no Hell, that it was an invention of religious leaders who used it to control the masses. But this place could easily qualify for that accolade, and I wondered if Albert had deliberately misled me in order to lure me to this God-forsaken nether world.

I mouthed a silent scream for Albert to take me out of this hell hole, but my plea was mocked by the deafening silence. So I floated in the blackness trying to stifle my mounting despair and wishing I was back on Earth where I could wake up from a good night's sleep and treat this trip as a very bad nightmare.

And now I understood why linear time does not really exist. In this environment I had no way of knowing if I had been there for minutes, hours, or centuries. Time had no relevance to me—it was a meaningless concept in the smothering darkness of this black hole.

And then I saw it—a tiny pinprick of light in the distance. I watched with mounting hope as the light got closer, expanding as it approached. When it reached me I floated through the opening in the blackness and entered the softly lit world on the other side. The only thing visible was a clump of small spheres floating in the middle of several rings of flashing lights that spun around the central cluster in erratic orbits. It was similar to the graphic of an atom I remembered from one of my science textbooks, with the globes in the center as the nucleus and the orbiting lights as the electrons.

Before long the image of the atom began to shrink as though I was being propelled backward by some cosmic force. As the atom became smaller, I could see it was one of many similar atoms that surrounded it, and eventually I noticed these atoms had bonded with other atoms to form molecules and compounds. As I continued my journey away from these tiny specks, I lost sight of the individual atoms and molecules as they merged into a large black globe made from a shiny glass-like material. Soon I could see that the black globe was the glass eye of a stuffed teddy bear sitting on a shelf. I recognized it as one of the toys our granddaughter likes to cuddle when she pays us a visit.

I looked around and realized I was standing in our family room. I could once again see the outlines of my astral body, and I noticed Albert standing beside me.

"Why did you abandon me in that awful black hole, Albert? And how did I get back here?" I said with pent-up anger.

"I didn't abandon you. I was always right beside you, even though I chose to be undetectable. I wanted you to feel what it was like to be totally alone in a sensory-deprived environment, so you would be better able to appreciate the joy of being in the company of other humans and animals on your planet. Your adventure in the black hole was intended to help you understand the crucial role your human senses play in your perception of reality.

"Your time in the black hole was brief—less than thirty seconds of your Earth time—but I think you will now have a different perspective about your human journey on Earth. My goal was to help you feel more connected to other people and creatures on your planet, and to Mother Earth herself.

"You left the black hole through an interdimensional wormhole that allowed you to observe the atoms and molecules that form the glass eye of the little stuffed bear. I wanted to show you that the space-time continuum is curved in countless different ways in an infinite universe that is always changing. Someday you will understand this fully, but for now you should reflect on your recent experience and use it as a steppingstone to achieve a greater awareness of yourself as a spirit having a human journey."

My anger with Albert subsided as I heard his explanation. I walked into my bedroom and slid back into my sleeping body.

The next morning I woke up with a start, until I realized where I was. I hugged my little dog, who was snuggled beside my leg, and rose for the day. Since my horrific trip to the black hole I did indeed see things from a different perspective. I noticed the soft texture of the carpet under my feet and marveled at the allure of the morning sunlight streaming through the windows. I stood quietly to listen to the cheerful song of a warbler perched in a nearby tree while admiring the intricate blending of pigments on the oil painting hanging on the wall.

I went into the garden to inhale the invigorating salt air from the nearby Salish Sea and paused to soak up the magnificence of the white lilies in the flowerbed. The lush green grass tickled my bare feet as I strolled under our apple tree, its branches heavy with plump green apples. Our little dog, Abby, bounded out through the open door in her puppy gallop, her ears flopping up and down in sync with the bobbing of her little head. I knelt down to rub her neck, delighted I could once again enjoy her company and the unconditional love she showered on me each and every day.

Albert was right once again. My time in the black hole had changed my perspective on life, and I was now keenly aware of all the beautiful things in the world around me. It was true what they say—sometimes we need to experience the darkness in order to fully appreciate the light.

I went back into the house and sat at my computer. I wanted to describe my journey to the black hole and then put it out of my mind.

Albert promised the next trip would be exhilarating, and I fully intended to hold him to his word.

Chapter Twenty-Six
The Birthing Sun

So far on my astral adventures with Albert I had met an assortment of souls on the Spirit Side who had lived many different lives on Earth. They were all at various stages of evolution, and a few had already achieved the exalted status of a Master. I knew I had lived hundreds of lives on Earth before this one, but Albert would not tell me where I was on the evolutionary ladder. He said it would be counterproductive for me to be privy to this information in my current life. When I left this life and crossed over to the Spirit Side, I could assess my progress as an evolving soul and determine at that time, in consultation with the Wise Ones, how many more incarnations, if any, I needed in order to graduate from the Earth school.

The thought of returning to Earth after this life was troublesome to my human mind because life here was no picnic. I understood that life on Earth was not supposed to be easy as it is considered to be one of the toughest schools in the universe. I wondered what it would be like to incarnate into a race of beings that had eschewed hatred and violence in favor of peace and harmony. Wouldn't that be a refreshing change?

Albert had scolded me often for whining about living on Earth. He told me I had freely chosen to incarnate on this planet, and I had no one to blame but myself. According to Albert, a life on Earth is regarded in a much different light when viewed from the Spirit Side. Because linear time does not really exist—it is an illusion on the Earth plane—a life span of eighty years is just the blink of an eye on the Spirit Side. So no matter how difficult a life on Earth might be, most souls feel it can be tolerated easily because it will pass by quickly with no residual carryover, other than the memories of the lessons learned.

Although Earth is a tough school, it is chosen by souls who feel they need to incarnate in a difficult setting in order to expedite their journey up the evolutionary ladder. In most cases only experienced souls dare to jump into a life on Earth, which means I likely enjoyed some soft lives on other planets before I started my journeys here.

When I return Home Albert tells me I will remember these prior lives, and then I will understand why I chose to enroll in the Earth school.

Albert had often told me that we are all eternal beings of energy that spun out from the Source like sparks of light from the central sun, and I wondered if the spawning of new souls was still ongoing. And how did a new soul decide where to incarnate? I decided to spring this question on Albert the next time he came calling.

"I have a question for you, Albert. Does the Source continue to spin out new souls? If so, how do they decide where to incarnate?"

"New souls are spawned on a continual basis, because the universe is constantly evolving and expanding, and the new souls allow the Source to fully experience what it has created. Let me show you this creation process in action."

Albert clutched my arm and pointed toward the center of the galaxy. The stars blacked out for a few seconds, then reappeared as we emerged beside a white star that Albert said was the birthing sun for new souls in our galaxy. I noticed a stream of sparks flowing out from the center of the sun, and as we got closer I could see they were balls of light floating toward a large planet that circled this star.

We followed this flow of light down to the surface of the planet, which was flat and barren of vegetation. The light globes had formed neat rows facing a larger sphere of light that pulsated in a rhythmic pattern.

Albert advised that the balls of light were new souls created by the Source as individual aspects of the Source. He said this planet served as the initial orientation school for the new souls, and the larger globe was a Master who was in charge of the school. According to Albert, these new souls had a great capacity for learning, acquiring knowledge, and accumulating wisdom, but they had no experience on the denser planes and needed a bit of sage advice about the incarnation process.

I listened to the lecture by the Master, fascinated by the whole process. The Master explained in great detail how the incarnation cycle operated and gave them a glimpse of what life on the denser planes would entail. The students were told how they could evolve as souls by acquiring knowledge and wisdom from their lives in a physical body. They were advised that each soul had to establish its own path and timetable for evolution by choosing the planets and life forms for its incarnations. The Master reassured them, however, that there was no such thing as a wrong path or a bad choice for an incarnation, because every life on the denser planes provided valuable lessons necessary for growth.

The new souls were given a brief rundown of the different kinds of life forms in the galaxy to help them choose their first incarnation. They were advised to travel to the different planets in the galaxy to observe their life forms in action, and to meet with other souls who had already experienced lives in those physical bodies. When they had picked the planet for their first incarnation, they would consult with the Council of Wise Ones for that planet for advice on developing their Life Plans.

When the lecture was over, Albert led me closer to one of the new souls and reached out telepathically: "Greetings, little one. I am Albert and this is Garnet. We are both souls who have lived as humans on the planet Earth. What is your name?"

The neophyte responded in a cautious voice: "I have not yet adopted a name, but like all other souls I have a unique energy signature that you can use as a frame of reference. I am impressed you both have incarnated as humans on Earth. According to the Master, Earth is one on the most difficult schools in the galaxy."

"It is not an easy place to incarnate," I agreed, "although it offers tremendous opportunities for growth. Now that you have been through your orientation, where will you go for your first incarnation?"

"I am not certain yet—I must explore a few planets before I make a decision. I will definitely not choose Earth until I have some experience living on the denser planes. Right now I am leaning toward a planet with a race of intelligent reptiles that live in peace and harmony with each other and all the other creatures on their planet. This would give me an easy entry into life in the physical world, something I can use as a steppingstone for future incarnations. I am very excited to begin my journey of exploration and growth, and I look forward to the day I can meet with you again to plan my first life on Earth."

The little ball of light sped off toward the outer edge of the galaxy, eager to begin its new adventure. I had once been in the same position eons ago, and someday when I could freely access the Akashic Records I would be able to recall the details of all of my previous lives.

As we journeyed back to my home planet I thanked Albert for allowing me to witness the birthing of new souls—the ultimate act of creation by the Source. Now that I knew how new souls were created, the inevitable question sprang to mind: What happens to the old souls once they have finished their evolution?

In response to my query, Albert had this to say: "The short answer is that souls never finish their journeys. They continue to grow and evolve without ever reaching the finish line, because there is no finish line. The Source and the universe it created are constantly changing and expanding, and this process will continue forever. This means souls can always find new dimensions and planets to explore and new life forms to inhabit, so their quest for knowledge and wisdom never ceases. All souls are on an eternal journey of exploration and evolution that has no timetable and no ending.

"Sometimes very advanced souls will choose to merge back into the Source for a short period to experience the ultimate form of oneness with the universe, although they always retain their own unique identities and memories. Refreshed from the indescribable ecstasy of this merger, they will emerge once again to continue their pursuit of wisdom and knowledge."

"This leads to another question, Albert. Since all souls are eternal and new souls are always being birthed, is it possible some souls will not be able to find a physical body for their incarnations because they are all taken?"

"This will never happen for a number of reasons. The universe is constantly changing and expanding, which means new life forms are created on a continual basis. And sometimes physical bodies are shared by more than one soul before they perish."

"Can you explain how souls can share one body?"

"As I explained to you before, the usual pattern of human incarnation calls for a soul to enter a newborn infant at birth and reside in that body until it dies. I also told you every soul has the final decision on when to exit the incarnation and return to the Spirit Side. A soul's decision to terminate its journey on Earth is based on many factors, with the most important being an assessment of the progress it has made to learn the lessons it had planned before birth. Sometimes a soul will decide on an early exit because the life it chose was too difficult for it to endure in its current state of evolution. Or maybe the soul is just eager to return Home so it can plan another adventure on Earth in a new body.

"Typically when a soul decides it is time to leave, it chooses an exit point—like an accident or disease—and it escapes when its body dies. But sometimes the soul will work out an exchange with another soul on the Spirit Side, so it will leave the physical body and the new soul, often called a walk-in, will take its place. This happens when the incoming soul believes the body about to be abandoned would be a suitable vehicle for it to encounter the experiences needed for its evolution. In other words, the incoming soul feels it doesn't need to start out as a baby and grow up into an adult, and its needs will be served by entering a mature body.

"Often this exchange is not noticed by the people close to the human in question, although occasionally it results in an inexplicable change in the personality and demeanor of the human who has received the new soul. Some people think the change results from a split personality, while others believe it is caused by illness or trauma. It is not easy for the new soul to fit into the new body without a few noticeable changes, and this can cause confusion and distress among its family members."

"The system works well for both souls. The soul wishing to exit is happy to accommodate the incoming soul because it has no further use for its human body, while the incoming soul can zero in on a life that will offer it the opportunities it needs without having to live through all the prior life events. The incoming soul will assume the remainder of the Life Plan that had been developed for that body by the outgoing soul, with amendments designed to focus on the needs of the new soul."

"Now it all makes sense," I mused. "I met a man recently who said he was a walk-in soul, occupying his fifty-year-old body for only the past ten years. He had stepped into his body on a soul exchange when he had almost died in a car accident. His family had noticed a change in his personality, which they assumed was the result of his nearly fatal mishap.

"The cycle of incarnation on Earth never ceases to amaze me, Albert. The Council of Wise Ones obviously has fine-tuned the whole process to ensure it runs like a well-oiled machine."

"This should not be a surprise to anyone," Albert responded, "because the Council has been overseeing incarnations on Earth for a very long time. Someday I will let you in on a few more of their secrets, but now is not the time.

"I regret to tell you this will be our last adventure together for the time being. I have other missions on my plate that require my attention, so I will leave you in peace to chronicle your recent adventures in your third book. I will be back sometime in your not-too-distant future to continue our astral journeys together.

"Before I leave you, I want to give you an opportunity to have some fun. Come with me back to the Spirit Side where I have a pleasant surprise waiting for you."

Chapter Twenty-Seven
Dance of Heavenly Bliss

We left the birthing sun behind and returned to the Spirit Side, where we strolled through the bucolic countryside until we came to a lake with crystal-clear water lapping up against a white sand beach. We sat on some beach chairs near the water, silently soaking up the peaceful ambience of this secluded little haven.

Before long a man in a white hooded robe appeared out of nowhere. He was a handsome fellow in his mid-thirties, with black hair, light brown skin, and piercing green eyes that twinkled with an inner fire. His gleaming smile lit up his whole face as he reached out to shake my hand. I had never seen this man before, but I sensed we knew each other.

"Good day, Garnet," the stranger announced cheerfully. "My name is Votan, and I am delighted to see you again. You don't remember me, but you and I have enjoyed many lives together on Earth. We are part of the same soul group, and our previous lives have been intertwined in numerous ways. We have been siblings and friends in several lives, but most often we were spouses. Sometimes I was your husband and you were my wife, and other times we switched these roles. Let me tell you about our last time on Earth together as spouses, which was one of my favorite lives.

"It was in the Mayan city of Tikal during the reign of Siyaj Chan K'awiil II, also known as Stormy Sky. I was learning to be a scribe under the tutelage of one of the royal scribes who lived in the palace. You were one of the ladies-in-waiting to the youngest daughter of the monarch. I first noticed you in the hallway of the palace not long after you began your duties. You were drop-dead gorgeous, and I was instantly enchanted. I couldn't take my eyes off of you as I watched you disappear into the royal chamber. Over the next few weeks I would often hang around the park where the Princess and her entourage would take an afternoon stroll, hoping to catch a glimpse of you.

"Then one day I worked up the courage to confront you in the palace and introduce myself. You were very shy and blushed easily, and I felt in my heart that you liked me. This was the beginning of a long courtship, and eventually we were married with the blessing of the Princess. We moved into a small house near the palace and lived a long and happy life together. We were blessed with three lovely daughters, who took after their mother, and our love for each other never faded, even during our twilight years. We passed from that life within hours of each other after losing our fight with malaria."

"What a fascinating story, Votan. I am sorry I don't recall that life, although I know I will be able to view all the details in the Akashic Records after I cross over here myself. Did you come here today just to tell me about that life in Tikal?"

"Actually no," Votan said with a sly smile. "Albert tells me you have been yearning for some fun and excitement on the Spirit Side, so I thought I would demonstrate what souls over here do when they desire a little ecstasy."

Votan stood up and motioned for me to do likewise. Then without further ado, he stepped toward me and merged himself into my astral body. It felt like Votan and I had somehow fused our spirits into one clump of energy. My whole body tingled with a surge of divine love that left me aching with ineffable pleasure, as wave after wave of orgasmic euphoria rippled through my body in a rhapsody of sheer delight. Every atom of my body throbbed with a heavenly bliss that infused my whole being with unbridled exhilaration.

It was a dance of ecstasy—a joyous celebration of unity with another spark of energy. A dance choreographed by the Source to ensure the souls it created can enjoy the magnificence of its universe.

Time seemed to stand still as we danced in the eternal moment of Now. And then it was over when Votan took a step back to stand in front of me once again.

"My God! That was awesome!" I exclaimed when I caught my breath.

"This is known as the Dance of Heavenly Bliss, which is quite common on the Spirit Side. It is a joyful and wholesome merging of two souls for a few blissful moments. It is a way of expressing our love for other souls, but it does not require a commitment or have any other strings attached. And because souls here do not form relationships like men and women on Earth, there is never any jealousy among souls. And unlike sexual intercourse on Earth, the Dance of Heavenly Bliss is done openly and without any embarrassment or shame, just as it should be."

"Now I feel a bit uncomfortable—because I am a heterosexual male and you are a man."

"Your secret is safe with me—you can hide in the closet as long as you want. But always remember this: if you don't swing both ways you will miss half the action," Votan said with a wink and a smile, as Albert chortled loudly at my side.

"Relax. I am just yanking your chain," Votan said when the laughter subsided. "Souls on the Spirit Side do not have a gender, even though they may choose to appear to others as male or female to reflect one of their favorite lives on Earth. Now you are a male on Earth, but you will lose your gender when you return Home, and then you will be free to appear as either sex or merely as a globe of glowing energy. I did not mean to cause you any discomfort, and I could have appeared to you today as a woman. I thought you might as well get used to our way of living here on the Spirit Side."

Albert was clearly amused by my reaction to Votan, even though he was well aware of my many inhibitions. I could have chatted with Votan for hours about our past lives together, but Albert signaled we should be on our way. Votan waved good-bye and continued his walk around the lake, while Albert and I strolled toward the doorway to the Spirit Side, both lost in thought.

The past few weeks with Albert had been nothing short of amazing. My astral excursions took me to places I never could have imagined in my wildest dreams. I had been on an emotional roller-coaster ride, running the gamut from sorrow and despair to jubilation and ecstasy. And now my tour guide was about to disappear from my life once again.

"Before you leave me this time, Albert, I have a question for you."

"Fire away, my friend. I am all ears."

"I have learned a lot from my recent trips with you, and I thank you for all your thoughtful insights about life on Earth and elsewhere in the universe. I am wondering, however, if there really is hope for humankind on my planet. Will my race be able to stop their violent and abusive behavior before it is too late?"

Albert looked thoughtful as he responded. "There is always hope for your civilization, but it is not a foregone conclusion. The Source created Earth and all of its creatures as a way to experience life on the denser planes, and it has been content to let life on your planet follow its own path without any interference. Unfortunately, your human civilization has strayed off course by allowing fear to rule its actions. And the only way to conquer fear is through love. If you can fully embrace love for all humans and for Mother Earth and all of her creatures, fear, and all of its spin-off emotions like anger, hate, and greed, will melt away like a snowbank in the spring.

"You have witnessed the unconditional love we enjoy on the Spirit Side and the peace and happiness that abounds on this side of the veil. This is a goal all humans should strive to achieve, but it will require a concerted effort by everyone on your planet.

"When you get back home remember what you have learned on your astral adventures and spread my message to all who will listen. The first day of the rest of your life begins tomorrow, so use your time wisely. I will be back before too long to continue our discourse, but now the ball is in your court. Go forth and tell your story to the world."

Albert took my hand and guided me down to my bedroom where my physical body was still sound asleep. Albert smothered me with a cheerful bear hug before rising up into the sky and disappearing behind the Moon. And then I slipped back into my body for another day on this planet we call Earth.

About the Author

Garnet Schulhauser

Garnet Schulhauser is a retired lawyer who lives near Victoria, on Vancouver Island, with his wife, Cathy, and little dog, Abby. After practicing corporate law for over thirty years in Calgary with two blue-chip law firms, he retired in 2008 and his first book, *Dancing on a Stamp*, was published in 2012. Since the release of his first book, Garnet has been active with book signing tours and speaking engagements and has been a frequent guest on radio talk shows.

In *Dancing on a Stamp*, Garnet recounts how his life changed dramatically one day when he was confronted on the street by a homeless man named Albert (who was actually a wise spirit in disguise—an emissary from the spirit world). This seemingly chance encounter launched a provocative dialogue with Albert who disclosed startling new truths about cycle of reincarnation on Earth and how we create our own reality through pre-birth planning and free will actions.

Garnet's second book, *Dancing Forever with Spirit*, describes his next encounters with Albert who guided him on a series of astral adventures to visit the Spirit Side, the Akashic Records, distant planets with fascinating life forms, and a human civilization that made the shift to the New Earth.

His third book, ***Dance of Heavenly Bliss***, continues the saga of his astral trips with Albert who takes him to meet Gaia, the consciousness of Mother Earth, two of Earth's mythical creatures—a Sasquatch and an Irish fairy—who live in fear of humans, and human civilizations on other planets that are very different from our own. On the Spirit Side he met many fascinating souls who regaled him with tales of their lives on Earth, including Moses, Jesus and his mother Mary, Lucifer, and the goddess Athena. These trips were designed to inspire humans to appreciate the diversity of life in the universe and encourage us to love and respect one another, Mother Earth, and all the creatures who share our planet.

Other Books By Ozark Mountain Publishing, LLC

Dolores Cannon
A Soul Remembers Hiroshima
Between Death and Life
Conversations with Nostradamus,
    Volume I, II, III
The Convoluted Universe -Book One,
    Two, Three, Four, Five
The Custodians
Five Lives Remembered
Jesus and the Essenes
Keepers of the Garden
Legacy from the Stars
The Legend of Starcrash
The Search for Hidden Sacred Knowledge
They Walked with Jesus
The Three Waves of Volunteers and the
    New Earth
Aron Abrahamsen
Holiday in Heaven
Out of the Archives – Earth Changes
Justine Alessi & M. E. McMillan
Rebirth of the Oracle
Kathryn/Patrick Andries
Naked In Public
Kathryn Andries
The Big Desire
Dream Doctor
Soul Choices: Six Paths to Find Your Life
    Purpose
Soul Choices: Six Paths to Fulfilling
    Relationships
Tom Arbino
You Were Destined to be Together
Rev. Keith Bender
The Despiritualized Church
O.T. Bonnett, M.D./Greg Satre
Reincarnation: The View from Eternity
What I Learned After Medical School
Why Healing Happens
Julia Cannon
Soul Speak – The Language of Your Body
Ronald Chapman
Seeing True
Albert Cheung
The Emperor's Stargate
Jack Churchward
Lifting the Veil on the Lost Continent of Mu
The Stone Tablets of Mu
Sherri Cortland
Guide Group Fridays
Raising Our Vibrations for the New Age
Spiritual Tool Box
Windows of Opportunity
Cinnamon Crow
Chakra Zodiac Healing Oracle
Teen Oracle
Michael Dennis
Morning Coffee with God

God's Many Mansions
Claire Doyle Beland
Luck Doesn't Happen by Chance
Jodi Felice
The Enchanted Garden
Max Flindt/Otto Binder
Mankind: Children of the Stars
Arun & Sunanda Gandhi
The Forgotten Woman
Maiya & Geoff Gray-Cobb
Angels -The Guardians of Your Destiny
Seeds of the Soul
Julia Hanson
Awakening To Your Creation
Donald L. Hicks
The Divinity Factor
Anita Holmes
Twidders
Antoinette Lee Howard
Journey Through Fear
Vara Humphreys
The Science of Knowledge
Victoria Hunt
Kiss the Wind
James H. Kent
Past Life Memories As A Confederate
    Soldier
Mandeep Khera
Why?
Dorothy Leon
Is Jehovah An E.T
Mary Letorney
Discover The Universe Within You
Sture Lönnerstrand
I Have Lived Before
Irene Lucas
Thirty Miracles in Thirty Days
Susan Mack & Natalia Krawetz
My Teachers Wear Fur Coats
Patrick McNamara
Beauty and the Priest
Maureen McGill
Baby It's You
Maureen McGill & Nola Davis
Live From the Other Side
Henry Michaelson
And Jesus Said – A Conversation
Dennis Milner
Kosmos
Guy Needler
Avoiding Karma
Beyond the Source – Book 1, Book 2
The History of God
The Origin Speaks
James Nussbaumer
The Master of Everything
Sherry O'Brian
Peaks and Valleys

Other Books By Ozark Mountain Publishing, LLC

Riet Okken
The Liberating Power of Emotions
John Panella
The Gnostic Papers
Victor Parachin
Sit a Bit
Nikki Pattillo
A Spiritual Evolution
Children of the Stars
Rev. Grant H. Pealer
A Funny Thing Happened on the
   Way to Heaven
Worlds Beyond Death
Karen Peebles
The Other Side of Suicide
Victoria Pendragon
Feng Shui from the Inside, Out
Sleep Magic
Michael Perlin
Fantastic Adventures in Metaphysics
Walter Pullen
Evolution of the Spirit
Christine Ramos, RN
A Journey Into Being
Debra Rayburn
Let's Get Natural With Herbs
Charmian Redwood
A New Earth Rising
Coming Home to Lemuria
David Rivinus
Always Dreaming
Briceida Ryan
The Ultimate Dictionary of Dream
   Language
M. Don Schorn
Elder Gods of Antiquity
Legacy of the Elder Gods

Gardens of the Elder Gods
Reincarnation...Stepping Stones of Life
Garnet Schulhauser
Dancing Forever with Spirit
Dancing on a Stamp
Annie Stillwater Gray
Education of a Guardian Angel
The Dawn Book
Blair Styra
Don't Change the Channel
Natalie Sudman
Application of Impossible Things
L.R. Sumpter
We Are the Creators
Dee Wallace/Jarrad Hewett
The Big E
Dee Wallace
Conscious Creation
James Wawro
Ask Your Inner Voice
Janie Wells
Payment for Passage
Dennis Wheatley/ Maria Wheatley
The Essential Dowsing Guide
Jacquelyn Wiersma
The Zodiac Recipe
Sherry Wilde
The Forgotten Promise
Stuart Wilson & Joanna Prentis
Atlantis and the New Consciousness
Beyond Limitations
The Essenes -Children of the Light
The Magdalene Version
Power of the Magdalene
Robert Winterhalter
The Healing Christ

For more information about any of the above titles, soon to be released titles,
or other items in our catalog, write, phone or visit our website:
PO Box 754, Huntsville, AR 72740
479-738-2348/800-935-0045
www.ozarkmt.com